Luke

KINGDOM NOW!

Here's to a new beginnings! together.

Graham x

2.4.05

By the same author:

- *What On Earth Is This Kingdom?* Kingsway
- *Gerald Quotes* Kingsway (available from Pioneer Direct)
- *Divided We Stand?* Kingsway
- *He Gives Us Signs* Hodder & Stoughton (available from Pioneer Direct)
- *An Intelligent Fire* Kingsway

Kingdom Now!

GERALD COATES

KINGSWAY PUBLICATIONS
EASTBOURNE

First published 1993

The following Bible versions have been used:
NIV = New International Version © 1973, 1978, 1984 by the
International Bible Society.
RSV = Revised Standard Version © 1946, 1952, 1971, 1973 by
the Division of Education and Ministry of the National Council
of the Churches of Christ in the USA.
TLB = The Living Bible © Tyndale House Publishers 1971.

Front cover photos:
Top: Zefa Picture Library
Bottom: John Wells/Science Photolibrary

ISBN 0 86065 978 X

Printed in Great Britain for
KINGSWAY PUBLICATIONS LTD
Lottbridge Drove, Eastbourne, E Sussex BN23 6NT by
Clays Ltd, St. Ives plc.
Typeset by J&L Composition Ltd, Filey, North Yorkshire

Contents

All stories in this book are true. However, the laws of libel towards the living appear somewhat virile at present. Stories about the dead may therefore contain even more truth!

My Thanks

It has been said that starting off together is a beginning; staying together is progress but working together and influencing one's time and culture is success. My family and many friends have not only stayed with me but made a vital contribution to the success and influence God has given our work.

I must therefore thank my best friend Anona, to whom I have been married now for almost twenty-six years, Paul our eldest son, who is now twenty-four, Simon, who is twenty-two and Jonathan, fifteen. We have shared family life and kingdom life together. Each of us has to some degree allowed the Spirit of God's kingdom and the principles of that kingdom to affect our lives together. We have not always been successful but we are still together!

In the small town in which I was born, Cobham in Surrey, England, we have endeavoured to be obedient to what God has revealed to us from Scripture and through his prophetic word. I am grateful for my initial Anglican upbringing. The credal statements and doctrine contained within the hymnology gave me an understanding of the nature of God and his kingdom. As a teenager, I parted company with the Anglican communion, a fact for which most are now profoundly thankful!

Years later, having been confronted with the gospel and having made a positive response, I lived my teenage years through the 'twilight zone'. I felt I was no good to God because I was too worldly but no good to the world because I was too religious! It was a lonely place to be. But after a near-fatal accident in which I was given four hours to live I joined the only evangelical church in our town, a small Plymouth Brethren Assembly which met in the Gospel Hall. It would be inappropriate if I did not record my thanks for the friendship, teaching and counsel they gave me in my late teens and early twenties. Without them I doubt whether I would be here today. They had a dispensational view of the Scriptures which was a massive barrier to my understanding of the kingdom of God in the here and now — but for just about everything else I am grateful to them. To Howard Fellowes, Frank Smith and Arnold Amess and the wonderful hospitality their wives gave me — you are fondly remembered and appreciated. The quality of your lives and your teaching of Scripture gave me a hunger for greater things — I'm sorry I disappointed you when it was found we could no longer walk together. Thanks too go to Bryan Price, my childhood pal, still in a Brethren Assembly, with whom fresh contact has been recently developed.

Being baptised in the Spirit and speaking in tongues in the late sixties/early seventies was not fashionable. Indeed, most people felt you had kissed your brains goodbye and rolled your marbles down the aisle. But twenty-two years later the Cobham Christian Fellowship (now Pioneer People), which started off with five people in my front room, has now planted out in Surrey's Farnham, Molesey and Byfleet, and urban London in Tooting, Wandsworth and Putney. Well over a thousand people are in those churches, which grew from that original five.

But we have always been a team. Without my friends Martin Scott, Stuart Lindsell, Nigel Day, my close friend and travelling colleague Noel Richards, Steve Clifford, Mick Ray and so many others locally, I doubt whether I would still be in the race. Together it is fun sharing the success and fulfilment of so much work we have done. Only space prevents me from naming others, no less worthy of mention. Your names are nevertheless recorded in heaven and you will be rewarded for your faithfulness and loyalty to the Lord and your brothers and sisters.

Our national Pioneer Team, which cares for churches, plants churches and trains leaders and evangelists, has embodied so much of our teaching. Not only embodied it but added to it enormously. John and Christine Noble, Roger Ellis, Kevin Allan, Pete Gilbert, Mike Morris, Steve Lowton, Stuart Bell, Ishmael, Dr Patrick Dixon, Peter Sanderson, Adrian Hawkes, Norman Barnes, Jeff Lucas, Jim Holl, Phil Vogel and Graham Cooke. Our 'staying together' has produced our 'progress'. Thank you.

I am also grateful to my two personal staff. Amanda Collins, both PA and secretary, who has typed this entire manuscript, deserves special mention. So does Rob Dicken who for over ten years has administrated Pioneer Trust. Thanks also to Martin Bleazard our new administrator. I appreciate your goodwill, faithfulness and loyalty.

And there are the others who have influenced me and allowed me to work with them. In the words of the apostle Paul, 'What can I say?' Roger and Faith Forster, Lynn Green, Danny Smith, Clive Calver, Cliff Richard, Bill Latham, Rodney Kingstone, John Barr, Mike Blount, Michael Green, John and Carol Wimber, Dudley and Ann Daniels, David Taylor, Maurice Adams, Dave and Pat Bilbrough, Ian Coffey, Errol O'Brien, Mike and Margaret Pusey, Stephen Strang, David Matthews, Anthony and Tanya Kasozi, Sandy Millar, Caroline Bonnett, Sue

Rinaldi, R.T. and Louise Kendall, Lyndon and Celia Bowring, Chris and Meryl Weinand, Rob and Glenda Rufus, Graham Kendrick, Nigel Swinford, Stuart and Marie Brunton, Norman Miller and Sheila Walsh, Tricia Richards, you have all enriched my life. Each has so clearly expressed and revealed the kingdom — now! To the local leaders of churches within our Pioneer network, you are in my prayers daily. Our respect for you and your work is enormous.

To every speaker who has sown important seeds and changed concepts that I fail to credit, you too are recorded and will be rewarded in the age to come. I would like to make special mention of the late Malcolm Muggeridge, and A. W. Tozer, as well as Bob Mumford, Ravi Zacharias, Barney Coombs, Pete Lyne, Charles Simpson, Tony Campolo, John Smith, Doug Barnett, David Alton MP, Terry Virgo, Ern Baxter, Maurice Smith, Ted Crick, Dave and Dale Garratt, Tom Marshall, Louw Alberts, and Ian Bilby — your lives, writings and words as well as your friendship have enriched my ministry beyond measure.

And finally mention must be made of the few who were my friends, who no longer share the same kingdom values and the network of relationships I've been privileged to work with. You influenced and enriched my life in our time together. Your departure from kingdom relationships and the commitment to the values you communicated so eloquently has convinced me even further that Jesus, and only Jesus, is worth following, wholly and exclusively.

Gerald Coates
Esher, Surrey
1993

The Explanation

The well known and quite brilliant Anglican writer and lecturer John Stott and I shared two platforms in the eighties. One, on a day when the majority of London virtually came to a standstill due to snow storms, nevertheless drew 700 Christian leaders together for a day-long seminar on the subject 'The kingdom of God — already — but not yet!' There were two main groups present, the Anglican and House Church. The event was liberally sprinkled (not theologically) with Baptists, Pentecostals, Methodists and Independent Evangelicals.

A short time later, John Stott was kind and courageous enough to invite me to his own conference, which as it happened was largely attended by Anglicans including a number of bishops' wives, who were unable to get into another major international Anglican event. The subject was the same. John gave his excellent paper on the balance between what is 'already' and what is 'not yet'. It was masterly. He acknowledged that God did heal and speak prophetically through his people. At his request I gave a sort of 'state of the nation' talk not dissimilar to what we had done at our previous leadership event. They were helpful days.

But what was the difference? It was not in the importance or the authority of Scripture. Our differences lay in a quite distinct area.

The kingdom of God is full of people hungering, thirsting and seeking; knocking on the doors of heaven and hoping to empty it of its truth, power, integrity and glory until we have 'heaven on earth'. It is an experiential Christianity we are talking about here, and one that doesn't always have a slick Bible verse for everything it does.

For example, Peter had no biblical precedent when people brought the sick to be laid in his shadow so that they might be healed; Paul had no Bible text for sending out prayer cloths for the sick. Certainly Peter couldn't readily find the relevant Bible texts when the Gentiles were saved, baptised in the Holy Spirit and spoke in other tongues! Of course, later on they did find odd verses at the end of Amos which put their experience into a new-found light. The Spirit leads us into the truth — although truth can sometimes be the gateway that leads us to the Spirit.

So often we experience the mercy of God, the grace of God, the truth of God and the ways of God before we fully understand them or can give coherent explanations from Scripture about them. So this is dangerous Christianity, but it is the only one the New Testament church ever knew! The Bible is a test book, not a text book.

Jesus didn't take his disciples through an academic course of the Old Testament, systematic theology, history and geography, with a little psychiatry and social ethics thrown in. What he gave them was experience, the gift of the Holy Spirit and revelation from heaven and holy writings. He gave substance, explanation and insight into the validity and purpose of those experiences.

My differences with conservative evangelicals as against charismatic evangelicals are focused in this publication. *Kingdom Now!* is about getting as much of the kingdom as we can. Now! Forgiveness for wrongdoers. Healing for the sick. Deliverance for the oppressed and demonised. The investment of resources into the poor and the marginalised. Jesus taught us to pray 'Your kingdom come, your will be done, on earth as it is in heaven.' This wasn't surprising as he went up and down the Promised Land doing the very things I have just listed.

Of course, there are many things that are 'already' and some that are clearly 'not yet'. They come after our Lord Jesus has returned to set up his kingdom on the earth: a kingdom rich in grace and truth, friendships and loyalty, faithfulness and commitment; complete with animals and streams, sunlight and laughter. We are not given many clues as to what the age to come is going to be like — but it is going to be something like that. The Scriptures tell us that much.

Nearly all the creeds either futurise the kingdom or have erased all mention of it, whereas Jesus made the kingdom imminent: 'Behold, the kingdom of heaven is at hand.' In the words of my friend Roger Forster, we can stretch out our hands and grab great big handfuls of it and drag kingdom life, kingdom spirit, kingdom truth and kingdom principles into our personal morality, our relationships, finances, business life, ministry and travels. The kingdom of God is 'at hand'.

God deliver us from 'behold, the charismatic movement is at hand' or even 'behold, the evangelicals are at hand'. No. This is something much larger than charismatic evangelicalism, it is the kingdom of God! That will be our starting point in Chapter 1, 'Kingdom Now? Or Not Yet?'

Sections of charismatic evangelicalism both in the denominations and the House Church movement (now called New Churches by sociologists) have plateaued. But the kingdom of God is vibrant, dynamic and expansionist. The kingdom waits for bodies individual and bodies corporate to embrace the King and his kingdom, who will pray in unison with heaven 'Your kingdom come, your will be done, on the earth as it is in heaven.'

Some of the ideas in this book you may recognise from my earlier publications *What On Earth Is This Kingdom?* and *Divided We Stand?* (both now out of print), but there are always new things to say over ten years on. At the close of *What On Earth Is This Kingdom?* I noted that the issues of miracles, social justice, women in leadership and ministry were deliberately left uncovered. They were early days in those areas for some of us and I felt unqualified to comment. But God is in a hurry, his kingdom is being extended all over the world. Revelation is coming through experiences of life, and not surprisingly from Scripture itself! So these issues are reflected in the following chapters.

It was the eighteenth-century preacher Jonathan Edwards who wrote: 'The task of every generation is to discover in which direction the Sovereign Redeemer is moving and then move in that direction.' *Kingdom Now!* is written for those who hunger and thirst after the justice and peace of God's kingdom — and who long to move in his direction — now!

It was Jim Packer who observed:

> If charismatics err,
> they err only by expecting to receive from God,
> whose face they seek,
> more than he has actually promised.

So what can we expect — now? Just what has God promised? I would suggest there are major promises for the church and its mission that have been left unresearched and unattended for many decades by the Western church. Our sophisticated approach to theology needs a radical rethink in the light of falling church attendance, ineffective evangelism in evangelical churches and the moral decline of the Western world.

Now I have to confess that some of these further writings may offend. But as A. Skevington Wood wrote in *The Burning Heart*, John Wesley noted, 'What is intended to offend nobody is apt to affect nobody.' Yet even in our disagreements it is important we seek to listen, negotiate, prefer the other party and honour those who see things differently from ourselves. As Jesus taught us, 'if a kingdom is divided against itself, that kingdom cannot stand. And if a house is divided against itself, that house will not be able to stand.'

So I can probably do no better than conclude this explanation with a quote from H. G. Wells—not a believer himself. I confess I relish quoting those who saw the kingdom not clearly, but from a distance. They could never be accused of flag-waving or partisan literature! He wrote: 'The most radical proposal ever presented to the mind of men is the proposal to replace the world order with God's order, the kingdom of God.'

Today, 2,000 years after the announcement of this kingdom, we ask, 'Can it be done?' If so, how? When? Why? How much is 'already' and how much 'not yet'? I hope this book will contribute in some small way both to the important debate and its vital eschatological consequences.

There will be failures even as we hold Scripture in one hand and friendship in another. Yet it is often our failures that civilise us — our successes and triumphs can confirm us in our worst habits. We should never be afraid of failure. It may shake our strong opinions, shame our arrogance and embarrass our pride. But God can often achieve so much more in our weakness than in our strength. 'The meek shall inherit the earth.' Perhaps the secret of successful kingdom people is the ability to survive failure.

1
Kingdom Now? Or Not Yet?

It has been said that two of the dangers which confront the church are, first, that it has a message that may change and, second, that its methods may not change! It is precisely this sad situation which has led to the vibrant, dynamic, and at times apparently arrogant stance of churches daring to receive and implement many of the ideas contained within this and other similar publications!

A while back, BBC television phoned my office. They had heard about growing evangelical churches, different styles of worship, and a non-religious approach to Christianity. They knew that churches being planted contained a whole new generation of men and women who were orthodox and traditional in their values but unorthodox in their style and presentation. 'We've had a hell of a job finding you,' the researcher commented. 'We can't find your headquarters!'

These teachings and remarkable activities had not come from the USA, South Korea, odd groups across Europe or from any other quarter of that order. They have come from heaven itself. It is God's kingdom. Therefore we shouldn't be surprised if God initiates and sustains that kingdom. His headquarters are not on the earth! He is the

Head of a body through which the King is making kingdom values and vision known. His activity, kingdom activity, is never centralised, but takes place wherever bodies, individual and corporate, embrace his kingship.

What is a kingdom?

I live in the United Kingdom. It is not united — and it is not a kingdom. In order for a kingdom to operate, properly and healthily, it needs two things:

1 A king (or queen) whose word is final and whose power is absolute
2 A band of happy subjects, who are keen and able to do the will of the sovereign.

No decisions Her Majesty Queen Elizabeth II has ever made have affected my family or me in the slightest. The power lies somewhere else. She has little power and authority of her own. Someone else writes the speeches, makes the decisions and deals with the troublemakers.

In major sections of the church, and one has to say the liberal section in the main, the message has changed even though the methods may not have. A while back the editor of a diocesan newspaper, known to me personally, was sacked for suggesting that his bishop was in error for allowing an American priest, who was blessing 'married' homosexuals in church services, to lecture in Guildford Cathedral. Gone are the times when you would be removed for being actively homosexual or an adulterer, denying the Virgin Birth, the deity of Christ, his substitutionary death on the cross or his physical ascension or resurrection. All of those are accommodated in a 'broad' church where they agree on just about everything, because they believe in virtually everything!

What's to be done?

So evangelicals, and particularly charismatic evangelicals, may as well come to terms with one thing. Up to the year 2000 and beyond we are going to be talked about. We will be talked about locally and nationally, in the corridors of ecclesiastical authority and on the pages of national newspapers. As one author wrote, 'There is only one thing worse than being talked about, and that is *not* being talked about!'

A return to the King and his kingdom will stir every local community, its media, commercial enterprises and industrial concerns. A return to the King and the kingdom will radically affect the world of entertainment, politics, education and medicine. A return to the King and the kingdom will bring about a clash of values and personalities, but primarily of spirits. The Spirit of the kingdom of God is altogether different from the spirit of the kingdom of darkness. Not only are they different, they stand opposed to one another!

Jesus and the kingdom

Jesus spent his entire public life teaching and preaching about two things: his Father in heaven and his kingdom on earth. Even after Jesus' death and resurrection Dr Luke informs us that for several weeks he gave himself entirely to 'speaking of the things concerning the kingdom of God' (Acts 1:3).

It is not surprising therefore that Malcolm Muggeridge, generally regarded as one of the finest authors and commentators of the twentieth century, should state:

> The question of the kingdom of heaven on earth and the kingdom of heaven in heaven does seem to me an absolutely crucial one. The appeal of Christianity as I understand it is that it offers us something beyond this world . . . Now it would

> seem to me that the churches and those who present the Christian religion to us have moved entirely away from this attitude and increasingly tell us that it is possible to make terms with *this* world.

Jesus in his teaching of the kingdom taught us that we should be 'in the world' but not 'of it'. That is, we should not separate ourselves from its colours, shapes, textures, smells, heartaches and struggles for we are *in* this world — God's world. But we should not be *of* its values, goals and motivation. Nor of its racism, nationalism and sexism.

The early church

In a sense, what happened 2,000 years ago was far more remarkable than we could ever imagine. They did not have 2,000 years of historical hindsight, experience and theological or eschatological understanding. Yet they followed a Man, some who knew him personally and others who knew him through friends. He told them that his kingdom was not of this world. Therefore they were not obliged to structure their thinking and behaviour to the permissive morality of the culture around them. Or of the court of the Emperor Nero. Or the weaknesses, cowardice and fear of his predecessor Pontius Pilate. Jesus was the King of another kingdom.

Today many churches are sailing under false colours. We all understand why we have denominations or particular groupings. Most stand for an historic and significant departure from the erring ecclesiastical status quo of the time. Each made a radical attempt at being kingdom people as against simply church people.

But we have to go back to the Christ before Christianity to discover the King and the kingdom. Scripture must not be understood through the church hierarchies. Hierarchies must be seen in the light of Scripture!

Of course, I appreciate that to a twentieth-century

sceptical mind and an all-embracing disposition these notions are fantastical. Idealistic. But as Derek Prince has put it so well, maturity is 'aiming for the ideal while living with the actual'. Immaturity is aiming for the ideal and refusing to accept or acknowledge the actual. Or, on the other hand, acknowledging the actual to such a degree that one loses the ideal. That is the tension kingdom people live in. The 'already' of the kingdom with its taste of forgiveness, mercy, grace, truth, healing, deliverance, reconciliation and justice and the 'not yet' which by its very nature has yet to be.

But the kingdom of God does not consist of dragging our past around with us, whether it be a dark and shadowy comfort blanket or an ecclesiastical waggon train. The kingdom of God consists of dragging the future into the present. Thankfully it is the meek, not the arrogant, who inherit the earth. It is the powerless, not the powerful. It is those who love their enemies instead of giving them their come-uppance. It is the poor who are blessed, not the wealthy. God's is an upside-down-values kingdom! We should also never forget that the faith of the followers of this King and his 'other kingdom' began not among brilliant intellectuals, the wealthy or the movers and the shakers. Not the academically brilliant, charismatic luminaries, the exciting or the beautiful. Certainly not among television personalities or leader-writers of Britain's *Guardian*, never mind *The Sunday Times*. It began among what many would regard to be the naive, the simple, the uneducated.

The announcement of the kingdom came to a peasant girl in a smelly northern town. To shepherds who didn't even have the right to testify in a court of law. Perhaps most amazingly, to astrologers! Our hymnology refers to them as 'three kings' while Scripture calls these star-followers 'wise men'. Where were the theologians? The media personalities who could do the holy child some favours? The powerful and religious who would make sure that the teachings of the Son of God would haul Judaism back to its God and its holy calling?

Of course, God knew that demonic forces lodge in the powerful, the religious and the hirers and firers of society. Therefore this gospel, this Christ child, was entrusted to peasants and shepherds, to astrologers seeking something beyond the stars. And each of them in their own way responded magnificently, profoundly and with reverential awe!

No, God does not believe in the goodness of civilised, rich and powerful humanity. He is aware of the ruling passions of self-preservation, which if threatened would rather have the child killed. That is why, 2,000 years later, one is always amazed at the powerful and to my mind pseudo-intelligent idiot voices prophesying peace, reconciliation and a new order by the end of the decade.

Forfeited innocence

We have seen communist utopianism throwing up Lenin and Stalin; the pursuit of the American dream with John F. Kennedy and Lyndon Johnson; the purity and mission of the Muslim faith in Saddam Hussein and the Ayatollah Khomeini; the holiness of Protestantism, American-style, with Jimmy Swaggart and Jimmy Bakker; and if that hasn't shown us the shallowness and stupidity of power, we have the largest 'Christian' organised grouping in the world, overseeing, funding and resourcing its entire operation — through an evil, corrupt and crooked bank!

Eternal words

It is religion, and Christian religion at that, which not so long ago sought to keep the Scriptures from the eyes of men and women throughout the world. Brave souls were burned alive at the stake, garrotted, put on the rack, disembowelled while still alive, drowned and all manner of unspeakable things done to them. For what reason? They wanted the words of Jesus, this good news for the powerless, to take its course through the nations of the world. They wanted the sayings of Christ to be read and understood by the lowliest in their land.

And this is just what the religious leaders feared, as they always do. They fear a Spirit-inspired people movement that may rob them of power! True Christianity has always been a people movement. And when any religion, 'Christian' or otherwise, stands in the way of God and the common people, he will remove whatever is necessary, to reach the hearts and minds of those people.

The Temple was a place where Scripture had been read, God's praises had been sung and sacrifice had been offered. But eventually, temple sacrifice, temple leadership, the temple ways of doing things became temple prejudice. In AD 70 that Temple was all but destroyed; the only thing left of it (a salutary sign to all powerful religions) is the Wailing Wall.

The kingdom proclaimed

If Jesus were here today I have no doubt he would also be addressing himself to the powerful special-people groups, media moguls and personalities and the influential of our time. What would he say? 'The meek shall inherit the earth,' he would still say. To believers dashing around from church to church and from conference to conference he would say, 'The kingdom of God does not come visibly, nor will people say, "Here it is," or "There it is," because the kingdom of God is within you' (Lk 17:20–21).

To those satiated by the benefits of living in the West, drowning in a treacle of stuff and belongings, Jesus would say: 'Do not be afraid, little flock, for your Father has been pleased to give you the kingdom. Sell your possessions and give to the poor. Provide purses for yourselves that will not wear out, a treasure in heaven that will not be exhausted, where no thief comes near and no moth destroys. For where your treasure is, there your heart will be also' (Lk 12:32–34).

To those who wonder about the immediacy of the kingdom message and therefore the messenger's apparent intolerance: 'The time has come . . . the kingdom of God is near. Repent and believe the good news!' (Mk 1:15).

Perhaps to those who feel they lack education and certainly to the pseudo intellectuals of our age: 'I tell you the truth, anyone who will not receive the kingdom of God like a little child will not enter it' (Mk 10:15).

To those marginalised by society who have been denied the benefits others take for granted: 'Blessed are you who are poor, for yours is the kingdom of God' (Lk 6:20).

To the self-effacing, who believe they are worthy of no good thing from heaven: 'Come, you who are blessed by my Father; take your inheritance, the kingdom prepared for you since the creation of the world' (Mt 25:34).

To those who believe that the kingdom is mediated through their theology and theirs alone: 'I tell you the truth, the tax collectors and the prostitutes are entering the kingdom of God ahead of you' (Mt 21:32).

Words for those who feel this kingdom theology and kingdom living is a narrow-minded pursuit: 'The kingdom of heaven is like treasure hidden in a field. When a man found it, he hid it again, and then in his joy went and sold all he had and bought that field' (Mt 13:44).

And whether Jesus meant a literal camel through a literal needle, or whether he meant the camel going through the 'needle gate' in the outer wall of Jerusalem, his words to those who believe that life is the accumulation of property, automobiles, clothes and all the paraphernalia that goes with that life style: 'Again I tell you, it is easier for a camel to go through the eye of a needle than for a rich man to enter the kingdom of God' (Mt 19:24).

To those of us who hide behind our denomination or 'stream' who have the name of Jesus and his designated title 'Lord', on our lips every other sentence: 'Not everyone who says to me, "Lord, Lord," will enter the kingdom of heaven, but only he who does the will of my Father who is in heaven' (Mt 7:21).

To those who are occupied with their own affairs and their own culturally formed values: 'But seek first his kingdom and his righteousness, and all these things will be given to you as well' (Mt 6:33).

And finally, to those who believe that this kingdom is so full of grace and mercy you can live how you want with whom you want, he declares: 'Anyone who breaks one of the least of these commandments and teaches others to do the same will be called least in the kingdom of heaven, but whoever practises and teaches these commands will be called great in the kingdom of heaven' (Mt 5:19).

For the dissatisfied, disillusioned and depressed

So if you have been looking around recently saying 'There must be more to church than this' — there is! It is the kingdom of heaven. Read about it, discover it, embrace it, for in so doing you will find the King of all kings, the President of all presidents, the benevolent Dictator of all dictators.

When one of our sons, the one of the three who has struggled most with the Christian faith, brought a friend home and disappeared up into his bedroom, we wondered why. Minutes later, his friend left with a bundle of clothes, several objects tucked under his arm and our son was stuffing some cash (the only cash he had) into his friend's hand. 'He is off to Australia with his parents but he hasn't got any clothes, any belongings, or any money — you have to help someone like that.' Our son himself had few clothes and few belongings and, as I say, little cash — but we were able to whisper, 'Behold, the kingdom of heaven is at hand.' That lad, through the weak, shaky faith of a 'just about' believer had been touched by heaven, the generosity of heaven, the love that gives and does not expect anything back.

For wherever we see goodness of that order we see something of the kingdom of heaven, even among 'unbelievers'. It was because of this that Jesus was able to commend so many who were outside of Judaism and virtually ignorant of the word of God. To use a phrase in current usage: the kingdom comes with words, works and wonders.

Makes you wonder

I remember a day not so long ago when pop singer Alvin Stardust phoned me. He had made a response to Christ years before but regarded himself as 'not a very good' Christian. He told me the story of a twelve-year-old neighbour, Lucy. She had been sick for three years, had taken thousands of tablets, specialists were baffled. I asked Martin Scott, one of our leaders, to visit the girl and pray for her. A few days later she went for a regular check-up. To the astonishment of the hospital authorities and specialists there was no trace of the sickness in her! They were obliged to write 'miraculous recovery' on her medical records, and did so. As a church, we were able to declare with laughter, tears and applause: 'Behold, the kingdom of heaven is at hand.' The girl was not a believer and nor was her mother, but that didn't matter. The kingdom of God was brought into that situation through the obedience of a member of the kingdom — in this case Martin Scott.

When the wife of John Lodge, the Moody Blues rock singer, phoned me, distressed and perplexed, she explained,

'John has gone into hospital; they don't know what's wrong with him, his arms are swollen up and his hands tingling and stinging. He has a 103 degree temperature.' The hospital authorities would not allow anybody other than his wife Kirsten, to go in and see him.

'Would you allow us to pray as a church on Sunday?' I enquired. 'Oh, I'd be delighted,' she said in a relieved tone. We were only going to spend two or three minutes for this in our programme for the evening. But we sensed we should give ourselves to much more prayer as a church. We explained the situation in detail and went to prayer in groups.

On Tuesday afternoon I phoned John in hospital. 'How are you?' I asked somewhat hesitantly. 'Well, to be quite honest, Gerald, I'm really well.' I confess I was quite surprised, even though we had prayed. 'Tell me, when did this change take place?' I enquired. He replied swiftly, 'It was on Sunday evening!'

The Moody Blues tour, which consisted of forty-eight major gigs across the USA was about to go down. Several had been cancelled already. But within a few days he was in New York with the band playing tracks from their album entitled *Keys of the Kingdom*. The band are not all Christian by any means and wouldn't claim to be. However, as a church we were able to rejoice for them all. 'Behold, the kingdom of heaven is at hand!'

What a bet!

While Don Cupitt tapers off into sheer incoherence; as religious leaders blabber about romantic ideals that are not even within the understanding of ordinary people; while the political left assure us we can have justice without the Judge of the earth; while the right tell us that the national growth product and a free market economy is the way to salvation; while shallow and unthinking people tell us that all religions lead to God; as Eros comes out of hiding and parades around without shame; as old Father Time hides his scythe, assuring us of eternal life; and as kingdom people are lampooned in the press; we can declare 'The kingdom of heaven is at hand.'

Blaise Pascal wrote of a bet on eternal survival or extinction. Musing over this choice, as he pointed out in his *Pensées*, it was obvious. You place your bet on the possibility of eternal survival through faith in Christ and living in a way that makes heaven happy. If you win, you win everything; if you lose, you lose nothing! Bet on eternal extinction and you never discover there is no God. But if there is, you've lost everything!

However, the evidence of history, of those who have so often worked for justice, peace and reconciliation — all these lead us to believe that this 'bet' is not a blind step of faith. But with heart and mind entwined we put our confidence in our Creator and embrace his kingdom. If it's true, you win everything, if not you never know you lost. But what a way to live!

So what sort of people are kingdom people? Is there a norm? What is the purpose of this kingdom? There is clearly another kingdom which seems to be on the winning side. How is it all going to turn out? These are the questions I want to address having provided a window through which we can gain insight into the King and his kingdom.

2

Pioneers Now — or Settlers For ever?

'I would rather be part of a live heresy,' quipped P. T. Forsyth, 'than a dead orthodoxy.'

Fortunately, we do not have to settle for one or the other. However, compared to the dry ecclesiastical orthodoxy and predictable behaviour of the religious status quo, it may seem that way at times! The church has been immobilised by several aspects of theology, corporate church legislation and deeply engrained attitudes rooted in self-preservation. It was Narcissus who, after looking at his own reflection in a pool, fell in love with himself, toppled over, fell in and drowned. Much church life as we know it has done precisely the same.

However, Jesus was no settler! In fact he was called the 'pioneer of our faith' (Heb 12:2 RSV). The *Oxford Dictionary* describes a pioneer as 'one of advance corps preparing road for troops; explorer'.

If we say we are committed to Jesus, we must be committed to the things that Jesus is committed to. One of the things he is committed to is to pioneer a way out of religion, all forms of religion, into the purity and simplicity of friendship with God and respect for the people and things around us. Yet Jesus knew that pioneers do not pioneer on behalf of themselves.

Many have followed their heavenly pioneer and with him have cut through the twentieth-century religious jungle, to develop new forms of fellowship, worship, prophecy, healing and what I call a non-religious approach to Christianity. There has been a real attempt to return to the Christ who lived and died and rose again — before Christianity. Those committed more to the kingdom than the King, to the church than people, to preservation instead of progress, cannot be pioneers. They will not close the end of this age or usher in the beginning of the new. I will explain that further at the end of this chapter.

Pioneers or settlers

But the settling church, marking time as it is, will not bring Jesus back to the earth. The Second Coming of Christ is not a matter of time, it is a matter of response. Response to what God is asking of us — now! We have all been lulled into a false sense of security and ease. The desire to go on and be different, to be a radical alternative, not only to the world and its value systems but to religious church systems, vanishes but ever so slowly.

But 'much is required from those to whom much is given, for their responsibility is greater' (Lk 12:48 TLB). God has invested a great deal into us as individuals and as a people; he is looking for a return on that investment. Or we could put it another way.

The Dead Sea is the largest hole in the earth. It is 1,286 feet below the level of the Mediterranean. It is forty-six miles long and ten miles wide in places. Around four million gallons of fresh water flow into that hole daily. But it is nine times saltier than the sea! The water evaporates under the heat of the sun and so the water level remains constant. Because of the salt density there are no fish, few plants and very few birds as there is no food for them. And the reason for all this? The Dead Sea has no outlet!

The church has a bunged-up outlet. 'Official' channels may be in existence at times, but for many, dosed with religiosity, they are far too narrow.

With a few exciting exceptions, most current preaching and teaching is largely that of comfort. Many hymns are full of assurance and consolation. There is also the inference that it is somewhat difficult to be a Christian and hard to make progress, never mind pioneer through the sophisticated jungle of the twentieth century. A 'good' meeting or service is gauged by whether or not it blesses us personally. We don't even mind an occasional challenge, but most talks are to do with internalising things rather than externalising them. To externalise something means change, flexibility, a strong will and a clear purpose.

Of course, the Holy Spirit does bring comfort. He does more than that — he is the Comforter. The joy of his presence is often beyond words — especially in times of betrayal, failure, loneliness and repentance. But many of the fine hymns that we sing were written in times of strong persecution. Today most of us are comfortable, proper little Christians and yet for many there is a deep hunger to be something more, to do something more, to play a part in history — rather than watch it go by.

There is a difference!

Pioneers view everything differently. And the reason for that I will explain at the close of this chapter. It is the vital difference between pioneers and the other group — the settlers. Settlers have a different agenda, and therefore different priorities. Settlers have a completely different value system.

SETTLERS	PIONEERS
Nearly always resist change, as a matter of principle. And they are proud of it. 'Things haven't changed here for over thirty-five years!'	Understand that change is the essence of growth. Growth demands flexibility so they don't get too committed to 'things'.
Do give themselves to God, but it is calculated and only up to a point. After all, God wouldn't ask them to do anything they didn't want to do, would he?	Daily give themselves to God, knowing that he loves to grant us the desires of our own hearts, but they also understand that God has desires that we can fulfil.
Are often diplomatic, though confused and afraid of making mistakes, continually stifled and seldom translate their concerns into action other than through institutional channels.	Are single-minded, experimental and experiential. They are unafraid of making mistakes, often do, and therefore are ready to apologise, learn from their mistake and move on.
Use 'church' language: meetings, services, tradition, constitution, headquarters, authority, balance, love (usually fear or sentiment in disguise), moderation, committees, and 'it can't be done!'.	Use kingdom language: heaven, hell, straight, crooked, narrow, broad, obedience, Scriptures, God's rule in all affairs, honouring the truth and sharing with others.
Are predictable, always on time, precise over tenth-rate issues (which they make into first-rate issues), are generally middle class and only relate to other middle class people. Cautious to the point of immobility.	Are unpredictable, less concerned about time but reliable, unconcerned about class and colour and only cautious when it serves God's purpose.

Ensure eternal life is to be safeguarded and their version of truth defended. Neither, it would appear, has any power of its own.	Ensure that eternal life is enjoyed in the here and now; it is not something we receive only at the end of our time on earth but something to be lived now!
Have a concept of God — he is a perfect gentleman, who never raises his voice, never interrupts plans already made, always agrees with the notice-board and has a number of attributes, some of which are definitely better than others!	Have no static concept of God but do have a living relationship. God is seen as gracious but not British, in the habit of interrupting plans made in his name that he has little to do with.
Talk about the Holy Spirit in a vague, sentimental and distant fashion. He is not actually expected to do anything and is positively discouraged from doing so! Hence the lack of miracles and specific answered prayers.	Are learning that the Holy Spirit is the dynamic, active, powerful agent of God on earth. He is God and is therefore to be worshipped and obeyed. He is on the side of those who love the truth and loves to answer people's prayers.
See sin as breaking with tradition, failing to observe cultural etiquette and abandoning cultural standards. Sin also entails doing anything differently from the way it has been done for decades. Some sins are more acceptable than others — like gossip, sectarianism, superior attitudes and denominational pride.	See sin as doing anything that makes God unhappy — or turning back from a course that God has already set. Making mistakes is not always sin. In fact the pioneer deliberately risks making mistakes so that the vision may be firmly planted in other people's hearts and minds and then be implemented.

Settlers have no expectation other than a repeat of the past. The church may shrink numerically, there may be a lack of Spirit-led leadership, few may ever get converted or join the church. But they would rather get smaller, sadder, older and blinkered — to the point of extinction — than change their way of doing things. They actually want church life to be predictable, even if it is boring and meaningless. Many of them would probably agree with A. E. Matthews' description of his own life: 'In the end I got so old and tired and weary of living, that I looked in *The Times* obituary column each morning and if I wasn't there, I got up!'

Outmanoeuvred

The church is full of brilliant but settled people who could so easily play their part in God's pioneering purposes. However, they are unwilling to make the necessary sacrifice to create a path on behalf of others — even their own children. So they become outclassed, outrun and outmanoeuvred by men and women who are daily absorbed by Christ, his word and his ways.

Pioneers on the other hand are willing to abandon anything which does not fit in with what is on God's heart and in his mind. This means we can never abandon love, never abandon truth, we can never abandon relationships or any of the things that are eternal. We are going to know one another in the age to come — the kingdom of heaven will be full of friendship. It is all there in the teachings of Jesus and in the Book of Revelation. Our role is to bring heaven to earth, the kingdom of heaven, through our personal lives, our relationships and the various structures that are set up, particularly to care for the poor, the homeless and the marginalised.

Whereas settlers become what others expect them to be, pioneers are being themselves. There is perhaps nothing more wonderful than seeing men and women being themselves before their God. God is always himself with us. He is never trying to be God, he is never trying to be good and he is never living up to other people's expectations. He doesn't want us doing that either.

Authentic spirituality can be summed up in one word — reality. Whereas settlers major on false reverence — unreality. Actually to revere someone is to do what they ask you to do, in the way they want it done!

Holy ground?

Religion is best seen in what is often called the breaking of the bread, Communion or the Lord's Supper. People creeping around with funny walks and whispering in hushed tones as though Jesus were dead! No dancing here! No party! Thanks to Zwingli, who formulated the idea that it is a memorial service, it is one short step from being a funeral service. The strange thing is that few have twigged that this 'sacred hour' has got nothing to do with what precedes it or follows it. Note the sharp words, strained relationships and unkind remarks uttered as families are getting ready for Sunday morning church. And then note the often critical or trivial conversation afterwards over lunch.

While in New Zealand on one occasion with my colleague Noel Richards, we saw this demonstrated in a quite remarkable way. I was the main speaker at a conference for several hundred people. Noel was leading worship. There had been extraordinary times of praise, prayer and devotion, with excellent musicianship. On one occasion we even saw New Zealanders standing on their chairs, their hands in the air, making so much noise it really was like a party!

Then came Sunday morning! I arrived just in time for the meeting to start. Inside every seat was taken. But people wore clothes we had never seen over the last few days. Shorts gave way to trousers despite sweltering heat, and the whole place had the atmosphere of a morgue. At the front of the congregation was a long table filled with many loaves of bread and tiny little cups of Ribena. The same musicians led worship but it was like stirring up treacle. Life had given way to death. Happiness to sadness. Reality to pretension.

What should I speak on? Whatever I did was likely to do nothing more than please or upset. I came to the microphone: 'Ladies and gentlemen, of all the meetings in the church calendar, this is the one I hate the most.' People looked on with disbelief. I lifted the net curtain off the table and picked up a loaf of bread. I remarked that the Last Supper was a meal, with meat, herbs and spices, bread and wine and observed how unlike this morning's meeting it was. I took off a piece of the bread and ate some.

With that, a whole group of people got up and walked out in disgust. 'Why are you leaving?' I enquired. 'We are all going to have some in a short while; I'm just having mine before you.' A few more got up and walked out. These were the same people who had been in the conference, who had been liberated in the areas of praise, worship and in response to teaching and prophetic ministry. They had laughed, clapped and some had cried their way through the conference. But this was an unredeemed area, it reeked of religiosity, and no doubt some of my readers may feel that my New Zealand episode was uncalled for and irreverent.

But what is the point of breaking bread when you are not even talking to anybody? That is not what breaking bread is about. Breaking bread has to do with our relationship with God and each other, it is a meal, it is eating and drinking together, in the way Jesus asked us to. This other thing is false, it is a sham and someone somewhere has to point it out!

'Doing it' is doing it

Settlers lay great emphasis on religious activities in the church: Communion, the Sunday school, Bible study — indeed a church is judged to be spiritual or unspiritual according to whether they 'do' these things. No one asks whether or not the Communion really is a meal of fellowship, friendship, sincerity and love. Few ask whether or not the majority in the Sunday school go on to be mature and adult Christians or whether there is another way of teaching children other than in a classroom format. Settlers will tell you all proper churches should have Communion/ breaking bread on Sunday mornings — and a Sunday school.

However, God is currently looking for men and women who will devote their imperfect energies and personalities to pioneer. He is looking for people who want to make their faith more relevant to the culture in which they live. We choose to be what we are, pioneers or settlers. 'I will [I choose to] bless the Lord at all times,' said the songwriter (Ps 31:1). 'I will [I choose to] get up and go to my father,' said the repentant son (Lk 15:18). God gives us grace to choose.

We cannot determine what this will mean or where we will end up as a result, but God does let us choose. 'Where the Lord guides he provides,' is an old and wise saying. We need not fear the future, for he is our Shepherd going before us, with goodness and mercy following on behind, as we refuse to settle but seek to pioneer.

The greatest people in Bible times and indeed throughout church history were all pioneers. We may not always be at the forefront of pioneering company, but it is vital that we are part of such company. We can be a part of the network of support relationships that invest into those who have been given opportunities to express God's love, with public profile, locally, nationally and internationally. We reinforce that network with our prayers, finances, friendships and by modelling the truth.

Faith for the future

Ten years ago, I wrote:

> I fancy that the Pentecostal, charismatic and House Church movement may find it more difficult over the next ten years than the non-Pentecostal, non-charismatic, anti-House Church groupings. 'Much is required from those to whom much is given' is as true today as when our Lord spoke those words 2,000 years ago. We who have claimed special revelation and knowledge will be held accountable to the Lord for that. If the newer groupings are going to settle for what they have got, within a short while they will simply be a better quality of settlers. If the traditional settlers continue to settle, despite the enormous activity of the Holy Spirit throughout the world, they will, in the end, find themselves resigned to faithlessness and to little happening in their lives and churches.

In many cases, this is sadly what has happened. Pioneering people have settled. But I want to appeal to the pioneering spirit of leaders, to the pioneer's roots, of people in the New Churches and in historic denominations, who have in the past paid a price and made things happen.

You can choose to model yourself on pioneers, a good biblical practice — Jesus being the pioneer of our faith. Or you can actually be the model — something much more difficult. Both are relevant.

There are many reasons why people settle down and build their own empires, monopolising both people and structures. God hates monopolies! He hates religious monopolies most of all! Even the nuclear family can become an idol and an empire. There are many who will use their homes for the Lord but would never give their homes to the Lord — he might require a move! Of course, we cannot make Jesus Lord, he is Lord. The issue is, what are we going to do about life in the light of his lordship?

Pioneering heroes

When Moses, that remarkable pioneer who was about to lead the children of Israel out of Egypt, faced God and was recommissioned for this task, he asked for God's name. There were many gods in those days. But God didn't give him one of the many names he gave to others, on occasion, to describe his nature, character and purpose. He simply replied 'I am' (Ex 3:14). In other words, when there is only one of me, you don't need a name! There is only one living God — the rest are in fact no gods at all.

An alternative rendering, and one which many favour, is 'I will be what I will be'. God will not be what we want him to be — he will be what he wants to be. Because his will is in his word, the promise is as good as the fulfilment — which Moses had to find out. He'd been promised a land, but died without ever going in. God looked as though he was a liar! But he is the living truthful God, the Lord of all, including history. Hundreds of years later when the Christ of God was transfigured with Elijah, Moses came from somewhere or other — and was transfigured with him! If God had said to Moses, 'Moses, would you like to drop in to the Promised Land now for a brief while — or be transfigured with the Creator and Redeemer of the cosmos?', I think I know which one he would have chosen. But God was doing more behind the pioneer's back than in front of his face.

In other words, the kingdom is not our understanding of the kingdom. The kingdom is not our vision of the kingdom. It is an altogether more wonderful, glorious and mysterious kingdom than we can ever work out in our lifetime.

Take another Old Testament hero, Abraham, who was told to look for a city 'whose architect and builder is God' (Heb 11:10). But his descendants couldn't wait. So they founded their own nation, built their own city and erected a Temple which eventually stood between God and his people. Anything that stands between God and his purpose will eventually be destroyed — even the places where praises have been sung and Scriptures have been read, taught and expounded. God allows us to build our religious temples, but he doesn't want those we build for him, he wants those we live in. Abraham understood that God's will is in his word, despite the evidence all around him to the contrary. Those of us in religious and 'churchy' settings must understand that, although we should not spit on our past, which may have nurtured us in the life of God, we should be pressing on for more of the God who is moving on.

The King or concepts?

We either receive Jesus and abandon our unscriptural concepts, most of which are immobilising both us as individuals and the church corporately — or we abandon the historic Jesus, create our own denominational Jesus and cling to our concepts in which we find so much security. Then we can settle well, till that day when we shall see him face to face.

Pioneers are not those with all the answers. They do not live with a hundred per cent certainty in all they say and do. But in the light of contemporary and biblical history, they look at God's word and ways, they look at those who embraced his word and ways, and put their faith in this Christ. To pioneer on behalf of others and to be satisfied that in some small way we have lit a flame that may have flickered in the darkness, bringing light to a few, is surely the most noble and purposeful way to live.

Having listened to so many voices over so many years, I've come to the conclusion that if there is no God, if there is no heaven or hell, if the words of Jesus are not true and his perspectives are as irrelevant as a disc jockey's opinion on politics, it seems to me that someone somewhere has built a vast stadium for an incomplete game of draughts.

Our world is structured with order and beauty. It is difficult to imagine its colours and natural glory are an accidental state in which hate, greed, abuse and crime can flourish.

An end in view

In concluding this chapter I want to keep my word and explain what I meant about pioneers viewing everything differently. This view is the result of their having an eschatological purpose. Most Christians come together on the basis of their ecclesiology — their view of church, their way of doing things together — and that is understandable. It is difficult to work with those who do not share our vision and at least some of our ways. It is easy to work together with those who share both our ways and our vision.

But I want to suggest that this is going to change. That this is going to be a decade of new alignments. All sorts of men and women, leadership teams, church groupings who in certain ways do things quite differently, are going to come together. Because they are pioneers and they have an eschatological view of all they do.

Everything we do should be assessed in the light of our goals. If John 17 (in which is contained Jesus' high priestly prayer) sums up his priorities, then relational unity is something we must seek to nurture. We must stop our gossip, deal with the negative and erase character assassination from our vocabulary. Instead we need to believe the best, pray for one another, even our enemies, or those who act like our enemies, on the basis of relational unity. Our specific and general relationships, near and far, should be an environment in which the blessing of God will rest. Psalm 133 makes it clear that where Christian people share together in a measure of unity, God commands a blessing on them.

Then in Matthew 24:14 we find Jesus, not praying but giving clear directions to his disciples. If the former was a high priestly prayer, the latter was a high priestly command. It was simply to 'go into all the world' and network the nations with the gospel. He made it clear that when we have done that, 'then the end will come'.

Heaven is local

Is there anything we could do which would be more noble, more meaningful and purposeful, than to bring an end to the rotten, corrupt system most people live in throughout the nations of the world and usher in a new age? It must start in our own locality, through a church that is mobilised to pioneer into every area of society with grace and wisdom as well as truth and a strong Spirit.

Eschatologically Jesus prayed that we would be one relationally, by the way we treat each other, believe the best of each other and work through our difficulties. That is to be true not only of people in our particular church but also of those in Jesus' church across the locality. Also of leaders whose profile may be high, many of whom are successful and appear to be without flaw, others of whom fail at times in small and major ways. Jesus prayed that we would be one as he is with his Father. And then he commanded his disciples who were one in heart, spirit and purpose (pioneers!) to network Jerusalem, Samaria and the uttermost parts of the world with the gospel. He explained that they would bring an end to the age of injustice and oppression — hell on earth — and usher in heaven onto the earth.

I am not talking about reconstructionism — imposing Christian governments on an unbelieving world. Righteous government does not create righteous citizens. I am talking about what Jesus talked about: salting and lighting society, networking our localities with the gospel. Then, as each church becomes a pioneering church, new churches will need to be planted where there are no pioneering churches.

The Scripture teaches us that God will come 'suddenly' to his temple, fill the house and return to the earth for his people — a prepared bride.

The kingdom will fill the earth. We network the nations with the gospel — Jesus pulls the net in and gets the lot! Judgement and eternal hellfire follow for all Christ's enemies. The Enemy therefore is keen to blind our eyes to our eschatological significance.

The Enemy

There are many pitfalls and hurdles that the Enemy puts in our way to make sure we never achieve those simple goals of relational unity and networking the nations with the gospel. If all of heaven is on the side of those who want to do the will of God, all of hell is against those who want to do the will of God. We need to be wise as to the hindrances to fulfilling Jesus' prayers and directives. In the next two chapters, I hope to do just that.

If pioneers do not pioneer on behalf of themselves, but others, how can we keep the path straight and clear?

3

A Kingdom Without Rules?

St Augustine of Hippo referred to the orator and the preacher as 'a vendor of words'. And a more heated vendor of words you will rarely find (especially the American television variety) than those who believe they have a God-ordained duty to tell other people how they ought to live in every area of their lives. They are the rule-makers of the Christian world; not only the standard-bearers but the standard-creators.

Of course, when people try to live without God they generally look for one of two things — fulfilment through power or fulfilment through sex: megalomania or erotomania. In the words of Malcolm Muggeridge, 'The raised fist or the raised phallus, Nietzsche or D. H. Lawrence.'

We live in an age, particularly in the West, where there is an absolute insistence that the only thing that matters is you, your health, self-awareness, body, mind, the ego — the real you.

Proper Christians

Perhaps as a reaction to megalomania and erotomania, there are sincere souls who — partly through Scripture and tradition and partly through their own weaknesses, indiscretions and limitations — live to ensure that no Christian falls into either mania! A mesh of well-meaning, apparently harmless and indeed creative machinery comes into place to ensure that the believer and the church of God stay on the straight and narrow.

Conservatives

But my position is that far too many things have been legalistically excluded from the 'narrow' that are not only permitted but positively encouraged by our Lord himself. As a result, much of the evangelical church has ended up with an unattractive gospel, where Christians are known more for what they don't do than for what they do. In the words of the quite brilliant A. W. Tozer, 'we have exported an unlovely brand of Christianity'.

Perhaps I ought to clarify my position even further. It may seem to be a rather strange step to join a club, for example, or some sort of special interest group, confident that you were going to challenge all of its rules and argue with most of its members. And yet, this is what it seems I am obliged to do. I do not know whether my call is from God, or from common sense itself — which after all God has given us. The gospel is full of rational propositions and moral idealism — though thankfully it is more than that.

In the quest for cultural relevance and moral idealism, have we as evangelicals forgotten the rational, common-sense gifts that come from God? This is particularly pertinent in charismatic circles of the church. I am totally committed to a charismatic view of the kingdom and therefore the church. To a charismatic view of our shared lives together and therefore of the individual life before God. But God is often credited with saying and doing things that are not in and of themselves wrong, just plain ridiculous! As somebody once said, 'If I give my son a watch, I don't expect him to keep asking me the time.'

It seems that many charismatics have been given a watch, in the shape of Scripture, friendships, common sense, hopefully a reasonably educated mind and yet apparently most of these things are no longer needed as people 'hear from the Lord'. This can be dangerous and creates another sort of legalism. Those who live by Scripture, common sense, debate, dialogue and friendship are viewed as less spiritual than those who apparently 'hear from the Lord' five times before breakfast. Christians, in order to be spiritual, should be sensible. That is why I am an evangelical, not a liberal.

Liberals

It was a long time ago that I came to realise that the liberal-minded of our age have more than an intimation of a death wish. They have successfully planted the seeds of death in our churches, helping to empty them in a quite remarkable fashion.

As a reaction to the liberalism which crept into the church noticeably after the Second World War and all its carnage (how on earth can there be a God of love when you've been through all of this?) there has been a strong tendency within evangelicalism to revert to legalism. Keeping to the straight and narrow way, with its rules, will grant you success and promotion — but flaunting these rules will shoot you to the top of the church prayer list.

These rules may be as minor as how you should come dressed for church (don't come with an earring through your nose, wearing a hat if you are a man, without a hat if you are a woman!) or it may be something quite different. For example, the right to be regarded as a bona fide church might be judged according to whether you meet on a Sunday as against a Tuesday evening. If you meet on a Sunday, you are a proper church of one sort or another. Meet on a Tuesday — well, you're a sort of fellowship and not a proper church. These rules and laws, this way of viewing people and their corporate behaviour, far from furthering God's purpose becomes a massive barrier to pioneering. But the answer to legalism is not liberalism.

Which way to go?

Concerned with the legalism of evangelicalism and what it produces, I discovered that the liberal-minded have no answers to our dilemma. One sees this in the media, which have been totally ruled by the liberal-minded, whether we are talking about the press, television or radio. One journalist I know was convinced that the UK demonic headquarters was Broadcasting House at the BBC. There you can talk about the most outrageous, non-sensical, fantastical and lewd, and be applauded. However, references to a living God (outside of God-slot time), never mind miracles of healing and answered prayer, are at best belittled as mere novelties and at worst are viewed with a measure of cynicism. I've had many years of first-hand experience to vouch for the validity of that perspective.

It seems to me that the liberal (and therefore in the main anti-evangelical) view of all things does not present us with a sequential series of problems, difficulties, crises and disasters; rather, it brings us face to face with one issue — and one alone.

It is the liberal death wish which, as I've said, is successfully emptying our churches across Europe and America and causing countless millions to lose faith in a living, loving God; in the historical validity of his Son Jesus Christ and in the integrity of Scripture.

The liberal-minded allow you freedom to choose on just about everything. This includes destroying your mind with drugs and drink, the encouragement to choose as many sexual partners of whichever sex you want — the same sex or otherwise. It has invaded our value system and affects how we see our hopes for the future. Over eighty per cent of sex scenes on television are of unmarried people. The liberal view of all things has encouraged this, and among other things the fast spread of AIDS.

A touch of ironic lunacy is added when one comes to realise that this 'Gadarene course' as one observer called it is directly linked with, to all intents and purposes, optimistic notions and visions. Heaven on earth. Peace, this liberal mind-set used to tell us, is always 'just around the corner'.

A lesson learned

If our society collects and stores video reels of television talk-shows, news bulletins and educational programmes; if it packs away copies of *The Times* and *The Independent, Time* magazine, *Cosmopolitan* and *GQ*; if it retrieves national and local radio programmes on cassette, it may do future historians a great service. Perhaps they will be collected, packaged and buried beneath the largest television station or cathedral which was dedicated to liberal views on all things from politics to religion, sexual morality to the poor.

Maybe, when our so-called civilisation has caved in, like all others who went this liberal way, a new civilisation will emerge. One day, digging among the ruins of a building that housed an altar or technical equipment, they will find this mass of evidence to conclude that our civilisation existed.

I wonder how many years it will take them to work out why this civilisation, so well placed to achieve its objective of feeding the hungry (having created the wherewithal to grow mass crops and produce remarkable foods from soya beans and the like); to house the homeless (with massive wealth at the disposal of the Western world making millions into millionaires and individuals into billionaires); to bring health and healing into society (having created miracle cures through the inventions of penicillin, drugs by the megaton, spare-part surgery and limbs made from easily available materials); to bring peace to the nations (through the learning processes and incessant discussions and summits on peace); I wonder how long it will take them to work out why this civilisation, with such fine liberal objectives, actually took an alternative course towards destruction rather than harmony, towards increasing despair rather than providing hope, towards disintegration rather than order, towards chaos rather than stability.

The archaeologist, historian and scientist may also note that the abandonment of traditional Christianity, with its ethics, respect for life and moral framework, was perhaps one of the main reasons for this 'Gadarene' slide. The conclusion they would have to come to is that unlike other civilisations, who were all but obliterated by outside forces, our civilisation tore its own heart out through its education system, medical practices and political policies.

Change and decay

Malcolm Muggeridge puts it well when he says:

> Thus did Western man decide to abolish himself, creating his own boredom out of his own affluence, his own vulnerability out of his own strength, his own impotence out of his own erotomania, himself blowing the trumpet that brought the walls of his own city tumbling down and, having convinced himself that he was too numerous, laboured with pill and scalpel and the syringe to make himself fewer, until at last, having educated himself into imbecility and polluted and drugged himself into stupefaction, he keeled over — weary, battered old brontosaurus — and became extinct.

It is therefore understandable that against this background Christians want to point us to the straight and narrow way, but conservative legalism is no alternative to liberal freedom. On the surface things may look radically different, but underneath there is another story to tell.

This can best be illustrated by describing a meeting I was asked to address many years ago. Aware of the liberal influence of the church and the alternative dangers of legalism, they asked me to address their meeting on the subject of 'law and grace'. I questioned the advisability of such a course, knowing what I would say and guessing what the probable response would be. They took no notice.

Law or grace?

There was an air of expectancy as the subject was announced. I addressed the dangers, lunacy and irony of liberalism. I then began to take evangelicalism to task for its 'other way'. I spoke about the lack of scriptural evidence for such things as 'quiet times', Sabbath-keeping on Sundays, teetotalism, worshipping according to a fairly pre-set pattern Sunday after Sunday. Not long into my talk, a man interrupted: 'This is nothing short of disgusting. You call yourself a Christian leader and yet discourage the very things that the Christian life consists of. If we don't read our Bibles every morning, attend every meeting we can and pray with our families, how will we maintain our Christian lives? I believe that every Christian should be up first thing in the morning reading his Bible and praying.'

A lady sitting next to him (his wife as it turned out) nudged him in the ribs, raised her eyebrows and declared somewhat loudly, 'Why don't you then?' The reaction in the meeting ranged from stifled laughter, to naive bewilderment to acute embarrassment. He had been exposed, banging the drum for a course he neither believed in nor indeed followed. He was afraid that if his accepted standards were not preached (even if they were not practised), his whole life would collapse. Keeping up the charade of what a Christian should look like was to him better than acknowledging that he didn't read his Bible every morning, pray with his family every day or go to every meeting and conference he was free to go to.

What this somewhat embarrassed man was doing was legalistically and aggressively defending and propagating what he felt he *ought* to believe as an evangelical. Faith in the ideal was better than living with the actual, even if the ideal was never to become very actual!

Truth or grace?

Jesus declared, 'I am the way and the truth' (Jn 14:6). He never hid things under the carpet. Truth doesn't need a carpet. God is after genuine holiness, not glued-on holiness. If we are not truly holy there is little point in play-acting at holiness. God is in the business of genuine love, faults and all — not cultural niceness. The Holy Spirit is able to bring conviction with integrity when we are not doing the things that make heaven happy, and in kingdom terms this is infinitely better than group pressure, which brings fear and condemnation — and little grace for those who fail!

Basically, grace means that God is doing something for me — whereas law means that I am doing something for God. All of us live with a basic philosophy, rooted in one realm or the other.

It is true that while God loves us as we are, he loves us too much to leave us that way. But God is not continually seeking to change us through pressure, coercion or placing unreal expectations upon us. It was Augustine who formulated the pithy and now quotable quote 'love God and do what you like'. Augustine was not commending Christians to follow their every whim and fancy. But our usefulness or ministry is what we enjoy doing — even though there is often sacrifice entailed in that. The alternative is to have the church filled up with people doing things they basically don't want to do, while all the things they are gifted and have skills for are 'laid at the foot of the cross' wherever that may be. Such a notion is certainly not found in Scripture.

All-embracing grace

Every letter Paul wrote begins with 'the grace of God' and every letter concludes with 'grace'. Paul never got over the grace of God. It is by grace we are saved, through faith; and at the end of history, when our Lord returns, when the kingdom of God has netted the nations, and a temple is built of living stones, a home for God on the face of the earth — there will be shouts of 'grace, grace' as the final stone is put into place. Jesus himself, the corner stone and the top stone.

We enter the kingdom through repentance and find grace to change our behaviour and do the things that please the Lord. It is then that we find that sin and wrong-doing are no longer an inevitability but only a possibility.

The church should be a community of grace and truth. John saw the 'glory' of the Lord as Jesus went about his everyday life 'full of grace and truth'. Some of us are full of grace but are short on truth — allowing all sorts of behaviour in our own lives and then in the lives of others. Some are strong on truth and sadly, by implication, the rules and legislation that go with truth, but lack grace. God may have been gracious to us despite our sin, corruption, uncleanness and dishonesty — but we happily zap people with verbal fire every time they have failed.

Law and the believers

So does God's law apply to Christians? Are the 'grace' evangelicals any different from the liberals? The apostle Paul, filled with the grace of God but with a background of law, wrote: 'The law has become our tutor to lead us to Christ, that we may be justified by faith, and now that faith has come, we are no longer under a tutor' (Gal 3:24–25). Paul is writing here to Jewish Christians schooled in the Law of Moses, or the Torah. Writing to Timothy on another occasion, he explained that 'the law is not made for righteous men but for those who are lawless' (1 Tim 1:9).

Yet despite this and many other scriptures, despite the emphasis and teaching of Jesus' ministry — forgiving where he could, cleansing where he could, choosing not to keep an account of people's wrong-doing — there is still a strong tendency within the church to impose legislation. To keep people looking like proper little Christians. But if you are going to have law you have to have policemen to make sure the law is adhered to. Judges have to deal with offenders. For those who fail with some frequency to uphold these laws, one needs prisons.

God's will — a tightrope?

We need to understand that the will of God is not a tightrope, it is a broad grazing area. A narrow way is only narrow compared to the broadness of the other way. If the will of God is a broad grazing area, and the creative genius of God is reflected in humanity, then there is plenty of room for the sheep to frolic and play and do what they have to do. Yes, of course there are boundaries, and to go beyond those boundaries is foolish. There are wolves out there that devour and destroy. But Jesus our Great Shepherd doesn't place us in a square metre of rich pasture to test our obedience by watching how long we will remain in the restricted area. He gives us the whole field!

There was once a woman who was married to a hard and unloving man. Her life with him was one of unremitting work and fearful obedience. He made a list of all the things she was to do for him in the house, and week by week she found herself unable to finish the many tasks or to please him. At length the man died, and the woman married again. This time her husband was loving and kind, gentle and gracious. Some six months after her remarriage, the woman found the list that her first husband had drawn up, and to her amazement she found that she was completing everything on the list every week. Out of love and thankfulness she was able to do what fear and guilt had made impossible.

You see, he has put his Spirit within us. The One who gave the law came 2,000 years ago and kept the law — not the man-made laws of legalistic Judaisers, but the law of the Ten Commandments: respect for God, for one's self, for friends and enemies and for the earth in which we live. The New Covenant did not come into operation until after Calvary when blood had been shed for the sins of the world. So Jesus fulfilled the law. But the law-giver who became the law-keeper says to all who will believe in him, 'I will give you my Spirit.' We *believe* in the Lord Jesus Christ, we *receive* the Holy Spirit. That is the scriptural norm.

If we live by the Spirit, continually responding to the grace of God, in relationship with others, then laws and standards are not needed. The same Spirit who caused the writers to give us the Scriptures now lives within us and can be trusted. The tendency for people to live by the Bible without the Spirit shows we often have more trust in the words of the author than in the author himself. It is not that things are true because they are in the Bible, they are in the Bible because they are true. The truth was the truth before pen was ever put to paper. The truth about God, his Son Jesus Christ, his words and his deeds were all true before the Bible was ever penned.

We can trust the Holy Spirit to lead us into all truth. Truth is sometimes a door that leads us to the Spirit but the Spirit will always lead us to truth and never to fantasy, delusion, myth or decadence.

Why the Bible?

But before we become lost in a sea of charismatic subjectivity we must thank God that he has given us the Scriptures. They have been preserved at a phenomenal cost and we should be grateful for the saints of old, known and unknown, who one day will meet us in the age to come, who ensured we had the Scriptures in our own language, in our own homes and in our own hands.

Nature tells you a lot about God. He has got taste: grass is green, not purple! Green is his favourite colour; blue is a close runner-up! The colours, shapes, textures and smells of creation give us a clue as to the nature of heaven. But when it comes to knowing about Jesus Christ, Scripture is our only record; even though there were Jewish historians and commentators who wrote of Jesus, it was almost as a footnote. It is amazing that Jewish books, written probably without the knowledge of Matthew, Mark, Luke or John, are in harmony with their own writings.

The Spirit of truth

But it is not sufficient simply to be 'Bible-believing'. Some of the most deceived people in the cults use the Bible as their text book. We must use it as a test book. As we are led by the Spirit, we can test our words and behaviour, our attitudes and understanding, by Scripture.

If I am flirting with my best friend's wife I may 'feel' it

is justifiable for all sorts of reasons, but Scripture tells me it is dangerous and damning. Another may feel that using petty cash from work for a personal benefit, or using the company telephone for personal long-distance calls, or perhaps even taking things home from work is justifiable, in the light of low wages or extra hours put in. But again Scripture will tell us we are wrong. It is a brilliant test book and for most of us, facing such simple issues in life, it is not complicated to understand. As Mark Twain quipped, 'It is not the parts of the Bible I don't understand that bother me. It's the parts of the Bible I do understand that bother me.'

Relational grace

So often in the church, grace only works one way. If I want to mow my lawn on a Sunday, apparently I should show grace to the person who feels it is wrong to do that on a Sunday. A person who doesn't mow his or her lawn on a Sunday apparently does not need to extend grace to me! 'One man regards one day above another, another regards every day alike' (Rom 14:5) is relevant here.

'But surely we shouldn't do things that offend people' is a very frequent and sincere comment. I want to suggest, however, that if we live with the concept of not doing things in case we offend, we will end up doing nothing! We will not live in the house we would like to, we will not take the holidays we would like to, we will not wear the clothes we would like to and will certainly not eat out or make a substantial purchase of anything — for fear it will offend people. This is not what the Bible is talking about.

Perhaps I should draw a distinction between two types of people who are likely to become offended by our behaviour.

1. The Pharisees

Let's deal with them! The people Jesus offended were those who knew how to live and had already decided how everybody ought to live. They had their standards and everybody else should live up to them. Unwritten rules and traditions about food caused the religious people of Jesus' day to strain out gnats from their food and drink. Jesus told them, certainly in a humorous fashion, that while they were straining out gnats in food, they were swallowing camels in the rest of their lives.

People like this are bad news, hindering the life and grace of the Lord Jesus. Of course he did not go out of his way to deliberately offend; he had better things to do than that. But in the course of blessing others he cut right across so many of their traditions. He healed publicly on the Sabbath in the Temple. Instead of using a bit of evangelical 'wisdom' and taking his sick patient behind a Temple pillar for a quick pray, he did it openly. Instead of asking the patient, now healed, not to shout or do anything Pentecostal and to slip quietly out of the back door — he allowed the person to leap and jump and shout and praise God in a most embarrassing fashion. It offended the religious people of the day. Imagine such a thing at Westminster Cathedral, or Canterbury, or indeed any other piece of religious territory that is more acquainted with silence and death than with the noise of life and miracles.

2. The weaker person

But there is a second type of person. Paul calls these 'weaker' people (Rom 14:1–2). These are not the aforementioned bulldozers, crashing around, creating debris wherever they go. These are people who have been genuinely weakened by society, damaged by their history and no doubt had various sorts of unspeakable things inflicted upon them.

For example, you would have to stretch Scripture quite a deal, apart from blue-pencilling parts altogether, to prove that it is wrong to take a glass of wine or a jar of beer on occasion. Jesus changed water into wine, and the wedding guests admitted it was the 'best wine' they had tasted in a long time. No party-goer would say that if you served them with a glass of blackcurrant juice! We are also exhorted not to get drunk but rather to be 'filled with the Spirit'. Paul doesn't say, 'Don't drink,' or, 'Only drink non-alcoholic grape juice.' If he were here today he would say no different. Drunkenness was a scourge in society 2,000 years ago, just as it is today. But as the old adage says, the answer to abuse is not non-use but proper use.

In the twenty-five years Anona and myself have been married, we have had many people living with us, some for several years and others for a few months. At one time we had a young man staying with us who had had problems with alcohol prior to his conversion. He had therefore taken the sensible line of refusing to drink alcohol of any type on any occasion. Now there was a potential difficulty. I have never had a problem with drink. I enjoy a drink at the close of a day, though I rarely if ever take a drink during the day. Jesus drank — in fact he may have drunk more than I do!

And yet Anona and I had a strong conviction that to drink, albeit at the end of a day, in the hope that our lodger wouldn't burst in, would be damaging and perhaps an indictment upon us both. So for a considerable period of time all drink was put aside.

Eventually he asked us why we didn't drink, as he had heard that we were fond of a glass of wine on occasion. Unlike other Christian leaders we were not secret drinkers, conveying one thing in public while doing something else in private. We had therefore become something of a novelty on the British evangelical scene, not only by drinking wine but by actually stating that we drank wine! Our lodger, having lived with us for some while, came to terms with the fact that he had been cultivating a fear of drink, dreading a sherry at a business meeting or social gathering. Little by little we introduced him back to drink and therefore back to moderation — which in this case we felt was appropriate. We are not here talking about an ex-alcoholic.

In other cases, it may well be that the person who has had a major long-term alcoholic problem should take a policy decision never to drink. This isn't legalism, particularly if his understanding of God's grace allows him to give others the freedom to do what he has chosen not to do.

The friend who lived with us was a 'weaker brother' in every sense of the word. He wasn't charging around telling us not to drink but perhaps if we had, would have said with some difficulty, 'Look, I know you are free to drink, I know you enjoy drink, and I'm in your home after all. But I do have a problem with drink; can you help me?' The best way of helping that young man was to sacrifice our freedom to maintain his walk with God. But this was a real situation, not a hypothetical one. It was a real person we would have been offending, hurting and causing to stumble — not a theoretical somebody out there who might fall. It is untenable to live that way.

Scripture clearly teaches that we must not use our freedom for evil (Gal 5:13). Grace means that we are free to drink and we are free not to drink. It means we are free *not* to do all sorts of things and free to *choose* not to, if it is going to help someone else in a given situation. Grace means we don't judge people for the number of televisions they have in their home, or how much they spend on their holidays; it doesn't continually question people's motives. Our choices in life are determined by so many factors. The number of children a married couple may have, the type of education for our children and what it may cost, the sort of thing we might spend our money on (an extension to the home, a smart new car or an investment into a Christian church or charity). Grace means that I don't judge people who do things differently from me, spend their money differently, choose as a married couple not to have children or choose to have seven of them!

Born-again Judaism?

Try to understand the heart and mind of the disappointed and bewildered Paul when he wrote to the Colossian church: 'If you have died with Christ to the elementary principles of the world, why, as if you were living in the world, do you submit to decrees such as "Do not handle, Do not taste, Do not touch"?' (Col 2:20–21). The Colossians equated Christianity, quite falsely, with reformed Judaism. The modern emphasis upon recognition of Sundays, a complicated holy calendar, religious buildings, the clergy/laity distinctions, is all a hangover from the Old Covenant and is crippling to the simplicity of pure gospel liberty.

Many of the early Christians do appear to have escaped this Galatian/Colossian half-breed religion. We learn this from the writings of one of the church fathers, Justin, in the account of his dialogue with Trypho, a Jewish critic of the believers' way of life. In his first charge against Christians, Trypho refers to their wicked abuse of the Sabbath:

> This is what we are most at a loss about. That you, professing to be pious, and supposing yourselves better than others, are not in any particular way separated from them, do not alter your mode of living from the natives, in that you observe no festivals or Sabbaths and do not have the rite of circumcision.

> And further, resting your hopes on a man who was crucified, you yet expect to obtain some good things from God while you do not obey his commandments . . . Have you not read that the soul should be cut off from his people who shall not have been circumcised on the eighth day?

Of course, the early church believers normally worked on Sundays with the rest of the labouring world, until Emperor Constantine set Sundays apart as the official holy day in AD 321. God bound Israel to his law at Sinai, but never imposed a special national day on Gentile peoples. One day in seven was all God expected of Israel, but in Christ he has provided not merely one day of bodily rest but eternal peace within himself and, in as much as is possible, with all people everywhere.

The resurrection

As I've said, it is true that Jesus carefully kept all the ceremonial requirements of the Law of Moses: circumcision, Passover and the like. But he observed these regulations because the New Covenant did not come into operation until after his death and resurrection. But he rose, ascending into heaven, filling pardoned outlaws with his Spirit of forgiveness, holiness, purity and hilarity.

Salvation thrives on life, not laws. Salvation begins with reconciliation, not regulation. The early church were together every day, not simply one day a week, worshipping and praising God. They didn't go to church — they were the church!

Grace and law will never settle for peaceful coexistence. One must be evicted. When the believer properly fulfils the royal law of love, for God and neighbour, that person renders the law obsolete. This is a kingdom of unending grace, not unending legislation. God's law is now written upon our hearts (Jer 31:33) and we are to enjoy and live in God's 'law of liberty' (Jas 1:25).

In the Pharisees' minds there were many, many commandments. They were all looked upon as God's word and therefore to be obeyed. The breaking of one law was the breaking of it all. They could not be selective. 'Cursed is everyone who does not abide by all things written in the Book of the Law, to perform them' (Gal 3:10). It is all or nothing. If one part is broken, all is broken. You can't bend the rules. You either keep it or abolish it. You can't have it both ways.

The role of law

Why the law then? The law was a temporary measure until Jesus came (Gal 3:19–25). The Jews were governed and disciplined by rules and regulations which kept them healthy and holy. It protected them against other religions, idols and other ways of living that were unhealthy, immoral and idolatrous. But these laws were not simply arbitrary. For example, God did not have a crusade against pigs! He didn't just choose that animal and make an arbitrary decision that they shouldn't eat it. The pig carried diseases, making it a dangerous meat to consume. God knew that, even though the people didn't. Today the pig is one of the cleanest of all domesticated farmyard animals. That is why Paul, who spent his lifetime striving to keep the law — both moral and ceremonial — was able to write that laws were 'weak and miserable principles', shadows of a better deal to come (Gal 4:9 NIV).

Writing to the believers across Galatia who had failed to pioneer their way out of Christianised Judaism, he informed them: 'For in Christ Jesus neither circumcision nor uncircumcision has any value. The only thing that counts is faith expressing itself through love' (Gal 5:6 NIV).

Is anything unclean?

The Jews fought for the law and their culture because they claimed it was given at Sinai at the birth of their nation.

Paul argues that his gospel goes back even earlier than that! It was announced to Abraham 400 years before the law was given (Gal 3:8–17). The veil or the curtain was down for the majority of people, but Abraham lifted a corner and caught a glimpse of the age that was to come. The law kept the Jewish nation with a distinctive identity until the Messiah, the Saviour of the world, stepped into history. In order to maintain this identity they had to be a people living apart from all other religions and nations. Therefore God declared that certain foods were unclean, whereas Paul later states that 'no food is unclean in itself' (Rom 14:14 NIV).

Mount Zion was set apart as a place for the people of God to worship the living God. God separated them geographically from other religions as well as culturally. Yet when the woman at the well asked Jesus whether it was the hilltop group or the establishment group which was acceptable to God, he told her she had missed the whole point of worship. In the final analysis, those who worship God must worship him 'in spirit and in truth', whether they are in an established building on or off a hilltop, or out in the open air without a building of any sort (Jn 4:19–24).

We get glimpses of this again when Jesus commissioned his disciples to go to Jerusalem, where their friends were; to Samaria, where their enemies were; and to the uttermost parts of the earth, to proclaim the gospel which was to cut through every cultural barrier. Jesus and his good friend the apostle Paul were keen *not* to keep the Jewish people separate, but wanted them to infiltrate the world, taking the message of reconciliation among all peoples, of all colours and all social classes wherever they went.

Grace to sin?

This gospel declares that repentant wrongdoers should be received and accepted solely on the grounds of the fact that Jesus became the substitute for the unrighteous, and took the full impact for all the wrong we have ever done. So apparently liberal was Paul, on the theme of grace, that he had to answer the rhetorical question 'Are we to continue in sin that grace may abound?' (Rom 6:1 RSV). It seemed a logical conclusion. If things are this good and it is all by grace and not by works — we might as well go off and do what we like. Let's go ahead and have a jolly good sin up! J. B. Phillips translates Paul's staccato reply in a marvellous British accent: 'What a ghastly thought!' (Rom 6:2).

In conclusion I therefore propose that it is unbiblical for modern-day people, who claim to be New Covenant people, to carry around the clutter of altars, special priesthoods and ridiculous outfits — an updated version of the elaborate Jewish calendar plus all the other minor but no less crippling legislation we have in churches today. We have made a false divide between believer and unbeliever, and even believer and believer.

Law is of course important in as much as it maintains a restraining influence on society. It also points out disobedience, selfishness and sin. In a Christian context, it can draw an offender to find forgiveness in the eyes of God. But we do need to understand that 'the law made nothing perfect' (Heb 7:19) even if it was perfectly kept!

So an inch in the right direction is better than a mile in the wrong one. The road to recovery is bound to be slow, but be encouraged. God never gets disillusioned with us — he never had any illusions in the first place! But he gives us grace for when we fail. As a colleague of mine has said so often, 'God collects failures; it is one of his divine hobbies.' He is a God who confronts us with truth, but keeps us with grace.

But what do we do when we sin? Is sin an inevitability or now only a possibility?

4

A Kingdom Free from Sin?

During the radical demands and movements in the early nineteenth century, a document was produced demanding constitutional reform. It began 'We the people of England'. Later it was discovered that the authors and indeed only subscribers were simply 'seven tailors of Tooley Street'! Other than themselves, they represented nobody and their words represented nothing.

Jesus did not claim to represent the thoughts, feelings and ideas of the earthbound. Rather, he represented his Father and what he referred to as 'the kingdom of heaven'. When Jesus spoke, even the uneducated had a way of knowing that his words carried authenticity, authority and integrity.

Jesus had a way of addressing issues which was in stark contrast to our values in the Western world. He referred to a broad road and a narrow road, to two men in a field, and highlighted the difference and eternal state of the two. Because his words were true, he was able to represent his Father in heaven. It is not that things must be true simply because they are in a holy book — but rather they are in the Book because they are true!

In other words, if no one had ever recorded the teachings

of Jesus regarding heaven and earth, heaven and hell and the lost state of humanity through sin, all of those things would still be true. Written words do not make things truer than they are already.

Violating heaven?

Jesus spoke of the kingdom of heaven and what and who is in it. He also spoke of those who violated heaven on the earth. He made it clear that those who persist in certain forms of behaviour cannot inherit the kingdom of heaven. We should not be surprised, therefore, that the Holy Spirit endeavours to make us sensitive to sin, its consequences and its final result.

Perhaps having lived without much of a concept of sin, when we eventually become Christians we are convinced we are sinners by nature. Indeed, the person who keeps confessing sin is often looked upon as being more mature or holy than the person who is in the main free from sin. Sin and repentance have been elevated almost to star status. Certainly, where sins have been committed against people, confession, humility and grace often make way for the power of God to sweep through that community.

Sadly it is fashionable in Christian circles to look upon sin and repentance as spiritual. Holiness is still highly suspect! John Wesley had the same problem. While preaching on the theme of Christian perfection, he had this to say:

> There is scarce any expression in Holy Writ which has given more offence than this. The word 'perfect' is what many cannot bear. The very sound of it is an abomination to them. And whoever preaches perfection (as the phrase is), that is, asserts that it is obtainable in this life, runs great hazard of being accounted by them worse than a heathen man or a publican.

Of one thing we can be sure. It is not spiritual to sin! The majority within the fold of evangelicalism would agree that scripturally the practice of sin is abnormal. However, most well-meaning Christians have an obsession with confession. We even confess things that are not sin, 'just to be sure'.

An impossible dream?

God has given us a life which cannot sin (1 Jn 3:6). However, we do not always live from the source of that life. Sometimes we live according to the inclinations and passions of the flesh. We have an ability not only to respond to the God who is both within and without, but also to what the eye sees, the ear hears, the nostril smells, the tongue tastes and our body can touch.

It would be helpful if we could understand that we are not sinners coming into sonship. Sonship is a biblical word (more to do with status in the family than gender). No, we are not sinners coming into sonship, we are sons of God right now! And we are being changed from one degree of glory to another. If we are to live by the Spirit, and be free from habitual sin, we need not only to know how to be led by the Spirit, and test our lives with Scripture — but we also need to know our Enemy. Why? Because this Enemy wants us to sin!

A learning process

Once a person has responded to the gospel, believed on Jesus and received the Holy Spirit they have declared war! They learn to love what Christ loves. They learn to hate what Christ hates. Some things, Scripture tells us, are absolutely right and should be encouraged and nurtured. Other things are absolutely wrong and should be withstood, denied and even exposed.

As we have already seen, the kingdom of God means coming under his benevolent rule; stepping into his grace, submitting to his word. The kingdom is of course much broader than our vision of the kingdom, it is more than our understanding of the kingdom and it is certainly more than our experience of the kingdom. Satan is, however, totally opposed to God's kingdom. Sin, he believes, will destroy the fruit of that kingdom. Make it ineffective.

So where does sin come from? Is there a defence mechanism? Is the source within or without? During the Second World War, Montgomery kept a picture of Rommel on the wall behind his desk. He explained he didn't want to put it in front of him — he didn't want to be looking at the enemy morning, noon and night! But he did want to look over his shoulder every now and then and look into the eyes of the man who was out there planning his defeat. We should do the same. As we become more visible, the warfare we are engaged in will become more intense.

Dangerous visibility!

Most of this book was written while Anona and I were staying with Sheila Walsh and her husband Norman Miller. They had previously shared seven years in our homes in Cobham and nearby Esher. Sheila has been in the USA with Norman for almost five years, co-hosting *The 700 Club*, watched by some twenty million television viewers, and her own *Heart to Heart*, which at times topped *The 700 Club* ratings!

It was an interesting time, as they had recently moved into a beautiful home in Virginia Beach near Norfolk on the East Coast of the USA. Together with our young son Jonathan we 'did' Bush Gardens (infinitely better than Disneyland in my estimation), a number of old colonial-style towns and a couple of cinemas, as well as *The 700 Club* and *Heart to Heart*, on which I was a guest. One remarkable experience was being stopped at almost every cinema queue (or line, as they call them!), in every shop, indeed anywhere we went, and being asked, 'Is that Sheila Walsh?' It must have happened twenty times on one day alone!

Recognition comes through visibility. As the Christ-centred church becomes visible in localities and through personalities, recognition is inevitable. But that visibility also makes us targets for enemy activity, either through human agency or through spiritual oppression attacking us from various sources.

Weapons of warfare

The other fascinating thing about our stay with Norman and Sheila was the nearby airfield and the wide assortment of aircraft which regularly flew overhead. Many of these neither I nor Jonathan have ever seen in any book at all! Harboured in the nearby quay were four large battleships and a plethora of smaller craft and back-up cruisers. Norman commented, 'During the Gulf War, the docks were a ghost yard. All military personnel, marine and navy crews, as well as the USAF, were out of the country.'

In the area of military conflict, attacks come from land, sea and air. Therefore, the Ministry of Defence employs its forces in three categories for counter-attack. Namely the army, navy and air force. A formation of supersonic jets could hardly manage to chase a group of saboteurs down a back alley! An armoured car division would not really be the best suited unit to fight enemy warships at sea! In other words, the defence system must match the particular type of enemy activity. This is true of spiritual warfare as well.

As Christians, everything we do in the name of Jesus, and in the Spirit of that name, engages us in conflict with opposing forces. There is no need to feed the current controversy about spiritual warfare. Spiritual warfare is about praying. It is about going out into enemy territory with the gospel. It is about filling our streets with the prayers and praises of Jesus (after all, worship and praise are only prayer set to music!). It is about giving a hot meal to a homeless person or, in the heat-soaked Virginia Beach area of the USA, a glass of ice-cold water in Jesus' name. It is not one or the other! It is all spiritual warfare.

Those praying do not need to take pot-shots at those doing. The do-ers do not have to attack the pray-ers. The marchers do not have to ridicule the preachers. Those who love the gospel do not have to show such remarkable disdain for those who want to come out onto the streets of our land to wash them with heaven in a spirit of unity and love. We are not meant to be fighting one another! The Enemy is somewhere else. Divided armies don't win battles.

The world, the flesh and the devil

One bishop many years ago made a helpful distinction between the world, the flesh and the devil. Let us look at these distinctions, considering first the world and its values and how, like a cancer, it eats into our own value system. Then we will take a look at the somewhat controversial issue of what the Bible calls 'the flesh'. Lastly, we shall look at the issue of the devil. Does he tempt us personally? If he is not omnipresent (everywhere at the same time) and therefore can't be tempting in many places at the same time, what agencies does he use to get his will done?

The World

My wife Anona and I have three sons. Paul, our eldest, brought a dog into our lives for several years. The idea was that the house would be safer with Tilley to guard it. But apart from Cliff Richard who occasionally visited, there was nothing worth stealing! However, while Tilley could sometimes be noisy, she was certainly no brighter than any other canine. Most of her noise was expressed as the family came in! If any thieves had broken in, she almost certainly would have taken no notice of them or, having allowed them in, would have probably acted as a guard dog for their tools. So much for security.

I'm not particularly security conscious. Perhaps that is why, on one occasion, my Brooklands Capri was stolen from the High Street in Acton while I was speaking in a meeting in a nearby venue. Neither am I particularly strong or tall. I have weight on my side but not altitude. I was the kind of person that acquired altitude very slowly throughout my teenage years. I am also a coward. My dentist's remarkable phrase, 'You may feel a bit of discomfort, Mr Coates', still strikes me as one of the greatest understatements of our time.

If you have come to the conclusion that our home, my car and personal well-being are at some disadvantage in the world in which we live, you are right! Security in the home has now been attended to, as has the car, but I still feel at a disadvantage in the dentist's chair!

Beautiful or terrible?

But despite thieves and official pain-inducers, cowardice and the subsequent disorder we all experience, the world is not totally depraved! It is God's world and one can see the beauty of creation in a hand-carved item, a painting, a piece of music, and a feat of engineering. The world is fascinating with its views, technology, history, fine foods and wine.

It is for these reasons that most of us seek to enjoy the world in which we live, whether it be through music, the arts and the theatre, home entertainment, do-it-yourself, gardening or motor mechanics. Needlecraft, knitting, painting or learning some new skill are all being taken up by increasing numbers of women.

However, Jesus explained that we are 'in the world' but that we should not be 'of' it. For behind the stories in the daily press and glossy magazines, and the amazing technology of the communications media, behind so much of that which is pleasant to the eye and ear, nostrils and taste, there are values and goals which we cannot share. This is worldliness. Throughout the world are major issues of injustice, including the Western world. For example, the essence of a class system is not that the privileged are conscious of their privileges, but rather that the deprived are conscious of their deprivation.

Talking to the BBC television programme *Forty Minutes* on the subject of prophecy, I noted that it was interesting that Jesus prophetically cast his eye down throughout 2,000 years of history. He did not lead us to believe that the accumulation of knowledge, the art of learning from our mistakes — such as the disgrace of the hungry millions — coupled with the advance of technology, would better the world in which we live. Indeed, despite all of those incredible skills, areas of development and so-called progress, he prophesied the complete opposite!

Living in the world as we do, we are caught between the privileges of our existence, enjoying its comforts and blessings, and fulfilling our responsibilities, particularly toward those who are marginalised, powerless and unheard.

Jesus knew that his followers could end up in one of two extremes. The first would be to disassociate themselves from a world which, despite its pleasurable aspects, was often selfish, unjust and fraudulent in motive and purpose. The other would be to so identify with it that they would adopt its values and goals, while finding themselves with a different set of values when gathering as a church. He was fully aware that people with integrity cannot live with this dichotomy for long.

The nature of worldliness

So what is worldliness? It is not what many Christians believe it to be. True spirituality cannot be assessed by the amount of money we have in our bank account, the nature and style of our home, or where we eat or what we drink. *Worldliness*, quite simply, is an attitude of heart which is expressed in the degree to which we are *bound to things*.

I was brought up in a council house. I had a state education. My family were often not able to afford holidays. After almost ten years in advertising and the retail trade I then 'lived by faith'. Some of our experiences of miraculous provision are recorded in my autobiography *An Intelligent Fire*. Today, after twenty-six years of marriage, the death of my parents, gifts from friends and income from my writing and broadcasting, we live in a home which is more than comfortable by most standards. I can afford to pay the bills, and both my wife and I own cars.

But it is wrong to assume that those who fall into our first income bracket and life style are less worldly than those in the more fortunate latter. The Christians who never open their homes to a new convert or neighbour, in case they spoil the furnishings, have a worldly heart. It matters not whether it is a council house or their own.

Worldliness, then, has a lot to do with our belief about money and our attitude to *things*. The apostle Paul said that 'the love of money is the root of all evil' (1 Tim 6:10 RSV). While Scripture indicates that Jesus had some nice clothes, was invited to parties and had funds for his apostolic team, there were times when he had 'nowhere to lay his head'. He was both enjoying and enduring the world. Enjoying it in as much as he created it, and was blessed by it. Enduring it because it needed to be redeemed back to his God and heaven.

But retreating from the world, its noises, cultures, tensions and disappointments into a cloistered and religious atmosphere is not what Jesus did, and nor should we. But we do need to face the fact that the world and its shared Christless ethos can pull us away from our relationship with God.

Doubt and death

Worldliness creates a low-trust climate. It doubts Christian people and motives, but rarely its own shallow hedonistic values. In fact the only people I have ever met who have never doubted have been ardent materialists or militant atheists! There is no room for doubt in either of those camps.

All the greatest Christians have at times doubted the existence of God, his word and his ways. That is because of the dark, confusing world in which we live. The materialists and atheists are 'grinding out their appetites' as Shakespeare put it so desolately. However, the moment we are born, we begin to die. That is why this commitment to things and the embracing of the old unreasonable values is so absurd. Recently, on a BBC Radio 4 programme with Claire Rayner and Don Cupitt, Rabbi Hugo Gryn quipped: 'Mr Cupitt, when Mr Coates and I pray, we pray to the God of Abraham, Isaac and Jacob — when you pray, you must pray to "whomever it may concern"!' The Revd Don Cupitt told me he no longer believes in God! To him, there is no room for mystery. Life is edging towards death.

The prospect of death either brings us to our senses, concluding that a creative force must be behind the order of the cosmos and the snowflake. Or it drives us senseless!

Prophetic madness

The philosopher Friedrich Nietzsche, having considered this question for many years, came up with the notion that God is dead. Interestingly enough he prophesied that two things would happen once this notion was accepted:

1 That the twentieth century would be the bloodiest of all time
2 That universal madness would break out.

Nietzsche himself went completely mad, probably as a result of his syphilitic condition, eleven years before his death in the year 1900. A prophetic sign? Yet madness is not the uncontrolled unreasonableness we often imagine.

It is not difficult to translate this madness into a practical lesson. I know of many people who are by any standards outstanding citizens. Regular attendance at Christian services and meetings, hearty singing and occasional prayers are all a part of their lives. But what values lurk below? One can believe in God privately, but worldliness keeps faith out of the public arena.

The root of worldliness is expressed when someone asks, 'Can I borrow your car?' Nearly keeling over, the owner of the car explains that it is only insured for them to drive. This barrier is erased when the questioner responds, 'Oh, that's OK, I'm insured to drive anyone's car!' Countering the response, the owner replies, 'Tell me where you want to go and I'll drive you.' The final chapter of the saga is concluded with the questioner observing, 'Well actually, I've noticed you hardly use it now as you go to work by train and I was wondering if I could borrow it to go on holiday!'

The fact is, certain people would rather their car sit idle, losing its value and blocking the drive, than be used wisely, sensibly and at times mercifully for others. You may feel that this is a trifling illustration; it is not. It is a window into a selfish heart.

I know others, who have been left large legacies, or have access to a private trust, or through hard work and wise stewarding have a high interest account in a bank, or investments elsewhere. Then when their car breaks down, or maybe the central heating system needs attention, they give off the notion that they have no money. They have actually convinced themselves that in terms of general income and expenditure there is no surplus. Their invested £5,000 or £50,000 is not there as far as they are concerned!

It is untouchable and is reserved for the future; it can't be used for their own affairs or the immediate needs of people around them. This attachment to money is dishonest and worldly. It's a part of the madness. It is a statement: 'I trust in things.'

What a pressure

We eventually become what we glory in.

> Don't let the world around you squeeze you into its own mould, but let God remould your mind from within, so that you may prove in practice that the plan of God for you is good, meets all his demands, and moves towards the goal of true maturity (Rom 12:2 PHILLIPS).

Being heavenly-minded makes us of great earthly use!

> Whatever is true, whatever is worthy of reverence and is honourable and seemly and whatever is just, whatever is pure, whatever is lovely and lovable, whatever is kind and winsome and gracious, if there is any virtue and excellence, if there is anything worthy of praise, *think* on . . . these things — fix your *minds* on them (Phil 4:8 AMPLIFIED; italics mine).

The world system — its media in particular — tells us that the good life, the satisfying life, is found in things. I was involved in advertising for ten years. The role of the advertiser is to rob you of your respect and sell it back at the price of the product. A splash of this, a drink of that, a drive in this and a set of clothes made by them, hair looking like this and bodies like that, freedom to buy what you want when you want — this is the road to success. All of these things may at times be helpful as they come our way through hard work, the blessing of others and the kindness of God. Once they become an end in themselves, we become hedonistic — worldly.

Pleasure should be a by-product of serving God; it is secondary to being a blessing to others. When the accumulation of things, finances and security becomes a goal in itself they begin to take on a life of their own. God wants us to enjoy friendships, financial resources and things, but without a permanent attachment. Not that this devalues things, but it puts them in their proper perspective. I applaud the efforts of conservationists, town-planners and the like who endeavour to maintain and protect our cities and rural areas from rape and decay. It is God's world and most of us would rather live in well-kept regency Bath than run-down tower-block inner cities. But pleasure and ease are not the goal of the Christian.

Proliferating confusion

'Render unto Caesar the things that are Caesar's and to God the things that are God's' is among the most profound of Jesus' teachings. But our role in life is to ensure that Caesar is stopped from making off with the lot! Caesar now runs most of our schools, hospitals and just about every other area of life.

The government does have a responsibility before God to maintain law and order and to defend our nation. But it does not have the right or responsibility to educate our children, care for the sick and legislate on matters without reference to God. We must deal with worldliness and make our faith in God (not things) public!

In Britain, I am told, we live in a post-Christian era. (I believe we live in a pre-Christian era!) We are not religious, just plain materialistic. America is different. There people are religious materialists. But this is the only difference.

The Western world also presents us with a world-view or a worldliness where only what we can touch is trustworthy. A living faith becomes clinical theology. Rich and enduring love is turned to debauched and lecherous sex. Finely honed wisdom becomes a science. Endeavouring to find some meaning to life, we ignore the truth. It is a crazy world!

As Christians we are called to think through issues and one does not have to be academic to think. We should not be fooled by the academic world. It is absurd to believe that for almost 2,000 years Christians were little more than cretins who believed in Christ and other fantasies. Then along came Darwin and hey presto, the truth was revealed. The truth is that we now live in one of the most credulous times in all history, withdrawing our faith from God and placing it in almost anything. The post-Darwinian world is not a happier or more meaningful world.

Even certain church leaders would suggest that the Virgin Birth was a con trick and the resurrection a trumped-up story to bolster a movement. However, these same people will accept New Age values and doctrinal propositions, however nonsensical, provided they are presented in pleasant and conciliatory fashion. Take Bronowski's *Ascent of Man* for example. About twenty years ago, this television series received universal acclamation from the intelligentsia, despite unproven and indeed unprovable conclusions. The infantile acceptance of anything new (providing it is not in the Bible) has occupied the 'educated' for years. With respect to Darwin, the only fact which thoroughgoing evolutionists forget is that the missing link is still missing! These ideas, however daft, replace Christ and his teachings.

The anti-Christ

The spirit of anti-Christ produces anti-Christ. Anti-Christ is whatever replaces Christ, wants his throne and his rule. The pursuit of knowledge Darwin-style, rationality Cupitt-style, hedonism media-style, or the New Age movement Western-European-style were all preceded by an anti-Christ spirit. All are now anti-Christ.

All over the Western world, academe, rationality, the accumulation of things and daft 'new' ideas now have shining haloes of their own. And where does Christ fit into all of this? He doesn't. He's opposed! The difficulty with the pluralistic approach to life, faith and religion is that it destroys all reasonable debate.

Today, providing your knowledge benefits someone somewhere, your accumulation of stuff blesses a few others and your highly subjective faith makes you feel good, it is almost sacrilegious to suggest that there is another side to this one-eyed monster. But the accumulation of knowledge has also divided us from one another to such a degree that the artist can no longer understand the scientist and the scientist the artist. The accumulation of things makes us insensitive to the unemployed, the elderly and the disabled, our consciences being soothed with merely an occasional handout here or an hour or two of voluntary work over there. The 'if it feels good do it' philosophy of the New Age (as old as time itself!) is a demand for rights without giving thought to responsibility.

So we end up with Boy George and his band Jesus Loves You into Hinduism because 'it is full of love and peace', while the singer states on *Wogan* that he nevertheless hates India with its injustices. Boy George has never entered the reasonable debate, that India is the awful place it is partly because of the unjust, despicable and quite intolerable caste system, which in my opinion is even worse than South Africa's old apartheid system. An attachment to things and personal, if pleasant, experiences makes us earthbound, blind to reason and worldly.

God loves the world

John, Jesus' best friend, wrote, 'For God so loved the cosmos [the world] that he gave his only Son, that whoever believes in him should not perish but have everlasting life' (Jn 3:16). God loves the world, it's his world. But that is different from worldliness, where the ideologies and the things of this world obscure the reason for our existence, making us blind, insensitive and arrogant when faced with the simple teachings of Christ for our own lives, our friends, enemies and the world around us.

The seducing spirits of this age, in drawing us away from Christ, enslave us to value systems which are in sharp contrast to the teachings of Christ. The only answer to worldliness is for the brain-washed mind to be renewed in prayer, through Scripture and fellowship. These put 'things' into perspective. They save us from universal madness. Don't let the world squeeze you into its mould. Be creative — morally, sexually and relationally.

The Flesh

So the world seeks to lure and entice us with anti-Christ values — in music and art, education and ethics, and in the accumulation of things. Exposure to Scripture, Christian fellowship and public and private times of worship and prayer, renew the mind, nourish the heart and challenge values that are all around us.

We now come to the contentious issue of the flesh. It is important to distinguish between the flesh, as referred to in the New Testament letters, and our human bodies. The body is not evil. It is wonderfully designed by our Creator. As C. S. Lewis commented, pleasure was not the devil's invention, it was God's invention — including sexual pleasure. The enjoyment of food to the palate, music to the ear, beauty to the eye and fragrance to the nostrils, as well as feeling to touch, was all in God's heart and mind when he created us.

However, we come under the dominion of sin when we act independently from God, allowing these appetites to rule us. In that sense our flesh will never improve, and therefore cannot be refined. Once we are born of the Spirit, our souls (that is our intellect, our emotions and will) are to experience being saved day by day. Our bodies await the ultimate redemption, when immortality will swallow up all that is mortal. 'Therefore we do not lose heart, but although our outer man is decaying, yet our inner man is being renewed day by day' (2 Cor 4:16). However, God never intended continual civil war between the spirit and the flesh. Being told we have two natures doesn't exactly help!

Before we were converted to Christ, there was little or nothing within us that found him or his teachings attractive. Certainly nothing that would cause us to praise his name, lift our hands or dance in energetic gratitude for his goodness towards us. Upon hearing the gospel and making a response, we not only find our past forgiven and our present condition cleansed by the blood of Jesus, but we receive a new spirit. We now have a new nature. It is one that can respond to God in faith, prayer, love and devotion. It is one that now wants to pray 'Your kingdom come, your will be done, on my part of the earth as it is in heaven.' A transformation is taking place. Our nature is now to love God, obey God and do the things that make him happy.

But we do experience the pull of the flesh, which is often at war with the spirit. But the Bible does not teach we have two natures. We have a brand-new heart, and a mind that must be renewed. We have a brand-new nature which is at war with other elements, all of which are on the outside, not the inside! But external elements can and do affect our internal thoughts and feelings.

Alive or dead?

When Paul wrote to the Italian believers at Rome, he explained this whole issue of the flesh. 'Consider yourselves to be dead to sin, but alive to God and Jesus Christ' (Rom 6:11).

It is true that in the time leading up to our conversion,

the Spirit of God gives us a spiritual appetite. After conversion that hunger needs to be fed and that thirst quenched. However, if we feed ourselves on romantic or horror novels, news bulletins, a steady diet of questionable music, cinema films and videos as well as superficial conversations, it is hardly surprising that we find difficulties following the Spirit and resisting the inclinations of our flesh.

That is not to say that many of these things are wrong in and of themselves, but they can become an unbalanced diet. The reason many people do not grow spiritually is because they feed themselves on the wrong things. So we need to train our faculties to appreciate the beauty of God's creation, read and absorb helpful literature and the Scriptures, as well as submitting ourselves to teaching, both public and private from friends and leaders.

We have already noted that sin is no longer inevitable, only possible, once we have become Christians. If we maintain a proper diet, we shall find the Holy Spirit committed to transforming us and we become a partner in that transformation. The Spirit's purpose is to present us to God 'without spot or wrinkle' (Eph 5:27). That is, without the spots of immaturity and adolescence or the wrinkles of old age and senility. The Spirit works to present us to Jesus and Jesus wishes to present us to his Father — mature. It is no good trying 'in the flesh' to be perfect. We must dedicate our imperfect energies and inadequate personalities to doing God's will. The end result of the spiritual life is not an unruffled personality, rather a life of openness and honesty, humility and grace.

Righteous choices lead to healthy emotions and a strong spirit. As Donald Grey-Barnhouse once said, 'You see to it that you do right and God will see to it that you come out right.'

Sex and the flesh

Whenever the flesh is mentioned, sex normally comes to most people's minds, especially young people and single people. For biological reasons it is often more so for men than women — though by no means exclusively. I believe this problem basically stems from learning about sex at school, college and university, as well as our television screens. Gay sex, unfaithful sex and promiscuous sex are all broadcast as normal and desirable. So many of our attitudes and values come from the media. There is also an almost total lack of education and teaching about sexuality in the local church.

It is not surprising, therefore, for people to be bothered by masturbation until they are married and it doesn't always stop then. God wants us to celebrate our manhood or womanhood and not be afraid of it. He wants us to give thanks for our normal sexual impulses and emotional responses, rather than deny them.

Over this whole issue of masturbation, we have to face the fact that the Bible is completely silent about it. Those who lived 2,000 years ago had all the same basic desires and inclinations of a twentieth-century human being. The New Testament (as well as the Old Testament) continually directs us not to get drunk, rob, murder and swindle. Few believers have ongoing problems in those areas! It is amazing therefore that one thing most Christians experience, to some degree or other, is not actually even mentioned.

To sin or not to sin

Roman Catholicism teaches that when you sin, you should confess it to the priest. Protestantism came along and explained that we only needed to confess our sin to God. Freud explained that there were no sins to confess in the first place!

The further we get away from one another the more

prone we are to deception. Today, certain misdemeanours, failures and sins are freely discussed and laughed about. Yet masturbation is still an embarrassing subject for most people. As a result of this ungodly silence we become connoisseurs of the unintended consequence.

And the consequence is: we become very confused. This confusion is seen most notably in someone like Jimmy Swaggart who, using his remarkable oratory skills, crusaded against every ill in society particularly in the church. But crusading can become a cover for failing to face up to our own personal holiness on the one hand or to a confused sexual identity on the other.

We understand life backwards, but as Christians we are called to look forward. I am looking forward to some clarity on this matter. Compulsive masturbation, simply for the purpose of self-gratification, with other people in mind, is wrong. It reduces those we think about to sexual objects. It cultivates a mental intimacy that does positive damage to friendship and fellowship. But masturbation for the purpose of self-control is something altogether different. The act in and of itself is not wrong. When someone is under pressure to the point of distraction, whether single or married, it is often best that they relieve themselves — for at that point no mental stimulation is necessary.

I know of many Christian leaders who have given counsel to people about masturbation who they later declare have been 'delivered'. But no one ever went back a few weeks or months later to find out. Of course there are people who have given themselves to habits who do need prayers for deliverance. Permissiveness precedes possession. But the issue is not masturbation.

Within or without?

All temptation comes from an external source. It is not surprising to find shapes and smells, colours and textures stirring up our feelings, rattling our nerve endings or swelling our glands. But it is not the evil thought that is sin, but evil thinking. An angry feeling can be redirected into prayer or a constructive response. But sustained anger leading to resentment and bitterness is something altogether different.

'Sin is crouching at the door' (Gen 4:7). It is no longer in the nature of the born-again spiritual believer to be wanting to do the things which cause Jesus pain. So we should encourage ourselves with our new motivation, for example by speaking to ourselves! Far from being a sign of madness, it is actually a sign of being filled with the Spirit. Indeed, we are commanded to be filled with the Spirit and then we are given a clue as to how that happens by speaking or singing to ourselves (Eph 5:19).

Of course there will be failures and shortcomings and at times even outright disobedience. But an acknowledgement of our foolishness, stupidity, ignorance or wilful pride, and an apology to the Lord and others will bring about God's forgiveness and cleansing. 'If we confess our sins, he is faithful and just to forgive us our sins, and to cleanse us from all unrighteousness' (1 Jn 1:9).

Scripture and the flesh

In the Old Testament, the main usage of the word 'flesh' has to do with the principal constituent of the human body or animals. There are references to sacrifices and also one's own body. 'My flesh shall also rest in hope' (Ps 16:9). A man and woman, married, are described as 'one flesh' and 'all flesh' signifies the sum total of human existence.

However, in the New Testament the phrase 'in the flesh' is often used (Eph 2:15; 1 Pet 3:18; 1 Jn 4:2). To be in this state is not incompatible with being in the Spirit or in the Lord.

The flesh for example may be defiled (Jude 8) and can

be purified (Heb 9:13). The flesh therefore is that earthly part of us with its lusts and desires. Not all these desires are bad. But if we focus on these we have a 'mind' that is concerned with the 'things of the flesh' (Rom 8:5). It is this mind which is opposed to Christ. Paul lists the darker side of the deeds of the flesh in his letter to the Galatian believers, where he says of the flesh:

> It shows itself in immoral, filthy and indecent actions; in worship of idols and witchcraft. People become enemies and they fight; they become jealous, angry and ambitious. They separate into parties and groups; they are envious, get drunk, have orgies and do other things like these. I warn you now as I have before: those who do these things will not possess the kingdom of God (Gal 5:9–21).

Paul continues, as though to help the confused, as to what is of the flesh and what is of the Spirit:

> But the Spirit produces love, joy, peace, patience, kindness, goodness, faithfulness, humility and self-control. There is no law against such things as these. And those who belong to Christ Jesus have put to death their human nature with all its passions and desires. The Spirit has given us life; he must also control our lives. We must not be proud or irritate one another or be jealous of one another (Gal 5:22–26).

We live in our bodies, but we are not to be motivated and directed by the darker side of our humanity. Should any of that ghastly list surface in our lives, then a change of heart, a choice to refer these back to God and for him to pronounce his judgement and forgiveness over them is the only course to getting back 'in the Spirit' and into the mind of Christ.

Summary so far

So the world is the sum total of cultures and peoples who are without God. Worldliness is adopting the confused, 'mad' goals and standards of a Christless and anti-Christ society. Renewing one's mind, to think and live differently, is a major key.

The flesh is that state of activity which is independent of God. Recognition and confession assure us of forgiveness and cleansing, because of what Christ did for us at Calvary.

The Devil

Self-disillusionment is the key to spiritual maturity. Confidence in God rather than in one's self places us in the realm of faith and the unseen. 'Faith is the substance of things hoped for, the evidence of things not seen' (Heb 11:1). We live by what we cannot see.

Therefore we have to accept responsibility for our actions and their consequences. Nobody can make us angry, it is our attitude to a personal situation that makes us angry and keeps us angry. Nobody can make us resentful, we choose to be resentful rather than deal with our attitudes. As moral beings, living in a moral universe, we will one day face a moral God and answer for the morality (or lack of it) in our lives.

Passing the buck started in the Garden of Eden, from Adam to Eve and from Eve to the serpent. It is seen everywhere today between business executives and trade unions, politicians and opposing parties, and is also seen in family feuds, indeed anywhere where there is human activity. But the Christian, and particularly the charismatic Christian, has yet another ace up the sleeve. When there is no one to blame for deeds, and where there is a lack of acceptance of one's own responsibility, there is always the devil!

Accepting responsibility

Cobham is about twenty-two miles south-west of London. Its population is mainly white and middle class. I was born there, educated there and I have lived in and around it for over forty-eight years. The church of which I am a part — a Pioneer church — numbers over 600 people. But we have always had a concern for church-planting. Groups have gone out to cultures similar to our own and several inner-city situations.

Our first inner-city investment was when twenty-five people left the leafy suburbs of our town and went into run-down Tooting. In partnership with the Shaftesbury Society, evangelism and social action were high on our agenda. It wasn't long before there were over 150 people meeting on a Sunday, which included the core team, dismembered parts of the body of Christ that found their way into the Christian community and over half who were converts to Christ with virtually no church background.

One Sunday morning, a Baptist minister, a friend of our Pioneer network, was invited to speak. By the time the meeting began the building was barely half full. Roger Stephenson, the main leader, went out to the pavement to find the police had blocked off both ends of the road, stopping the flow of pedestrians and traffic. Not having sufficient time to find out what was happening, they began to worship and people slowly trickled in.

Half an hour or so later, he glanced up to the first floor where their offices were. Behind the net curtains covering the windows he saw police in flack jackets armed with pistols and rifles. Paul, one of the leaders, went to find out what was going on. The police responded: 'A man has just shot and injured somebody and has escaped into your meeting. It is vital you separate your congregation from this man.'

Roger had a brain-wave, a stroke of luck, or a word of

wisdom — depending on your theology! It was also a morning for baptism. 'We are now about to baptise several people,' he explained, 'so if you are a regular member of this church or you have been brought by a regular member of this church, do come forward and stand round the baptistry.' With that, the entire body of people moved forward as one, leaving a solitary soul sitting in the middle of the block of chairs.

The police moved in swiftly and hauled him out, without the congregation being aware of what had gone on. The police had got their man: the trouble was — it was the wrong man! The police had to acknowledge they had made a mistake, for although powers of darkness had been at work, they had assessed the situation wrongly. Roger and several of his team went and paid a pastoral visit to the poor man who had come to church looking for meaning to life and had left being bundled into a black Maria!

But was the devil to blame? It was possible that attempted murder had been committed. An innocent had been temporarily blamed. Or are these things just human nature?

Some clarification

On BBC Radio 4's *Sunday Programme* several years ago, I was being interviewed about the possible dangers of Hallowe'en. A witch and a professor were part of the interview. After the witch had explained what she was up to, the interviewer turned to the Anglican professor, who basically said that all this was nonsense and there were no such things as demons, indeed it is dangerous to personify evil. He went on to explain that evil is found in the structures of society and if only we could change those structures all would be well. Sweden came to my mind at the time!

I responded, 'It's a real shame you weren't around when

Jesus was here. He went around casting out demons. You could have told him they didn't exist and he was wasting his time!' I added, 'You should be ashamed of yourself, and you a member of the General Synod as well!'

The powers of darkness represent all that is within the realm of the demonic world. Scripture tells us that the devil is proud and an arch-deceiver. He loves darkness.

There is the darkness of sin. Scripture explains that we 'love darkness rather than light' quite simply because 'our deeds are evil' (Jn 3:19). There is also the darkness of ignorance. Teaching brings light and wisdom to those darkened by a lack of knowledge (Ps 119:32). Then there is the darkness of demonic powers (Acts 16:16–19). It is difficult to see in the dark, to make decisions in the dark and to find any meaning in darkness.

Out of control?

Linda had been a Christian for several years. Although she had been meeting with our church regularly, many fears had lain dormant and unconfessed. She was afraid of walking in the dark, what other people thought of her, of ghosts and demons. Later she confessed she was afraid of God because 'you cannot see him'.

One evening a number of us were spending time in worship and prayer. She began to weep. Another girl and I took her into the adjoining room. I had this immediate sense that this was not normal fear. Scripture teaches that there is no fear in love. Most fearful people just need a massive dose of the love of God, and that is obviously expressed through friendship, prayer, acceptance and approval. There is no fear in love.

'Linda,' I enquired, 'do you want to be free of this fear?' Through her tears she sobbed, 'I do, I do.' I unwisely closed my eyes and began to pray quietly. (Demons are not afraid of noise!) I reminded her of God's love and then

I took authority over this spirit of fear in the name of Jesus. There was a piercing scream and I looked up to find Linda bearing down on me, her face contorted, with fingers outstretched about to claw out my eyes. I had no time to think up a quick prayer. I raised myself up from the chair and addressed the demonic force in tongues. 'Out!' I reacted. With that, she slumped back into her chair. Colour came back to her face. I was shaking like a crocodile in a handbag factory! 'Are you OK?' I asked anxiously. 'Oh yes, I'm fine now, fine,' she replied. I nervously joked, 'You should have seen your face!' As quick as a flash she replied with a smile, 'You should have seen yours!'

Demons know that permissiveness precedes possession. If you permit yourself to do things which create a disrespect for God, for yourself, for friends and even enemies — the spirit world can latch on to that. Whereas previously you had control over the situation, once demonic forces lay hold they take increasing control of that area of life.

The body of Christ

Being in Christ also means being a part of his body of believers. Isolation from the Christian community, a sense of 'I can make it on my own', leaves us wide open to such forces. Whereas God says 'I am' the devil likes to say 'I am not'. He doesn't particularly want unbelievers to believe in him and he certainly doesn't want backslidden, disenfranchised or disillusioned believers to imagine he has any control on their lives. But inevitably he does. He takes advantage of us in our tiredness and disillusionment, sometimes with our doubts and questions.

Submitting to God and his word is an act of the will. Those cultivated, fear-formed attitudes of Linda's could and should have been shared with others, and such an encounter would have been unnecessary. John, Jesus' best friend, summed up our safety with the words 'Greater is he who is in you than he who is in the world' (1 Jn 4:4).

It is amazing how many believers there are in churches who don't teach orthodox faith and orthodox behaviour and would not even want to call themselves evangelicals. They are sitting under a steady stream of religious platitudes and faith-devouring philosophies which, while clothed with religion and biblical phrases, are devoid of faith and the powerful Holy Spirit. Spiritual warfare is a game, evangelism therefore non-existent and generally speaking the leaders of such churches are planning for its demise.

'Submit yourselves therefore to God. Resist the devil and he will flee from you' (Jas 4:7). That is as valid today in our sophisticated twentieth century as it was in Israel 2,000 years ago.

The reason that the Scriptures and fellowship with others appear so important is that they give us certainty in our uncertain times. They draw our focus away from ourselves and from the world, away from fleshly inclinations and demons, to focus and find faith and live out that faith in our culture.

I believe in the body of Christ because heaven does. I believe in the church because God does. I believe every Christian should be a part of a community to release their skills and abilities, to protect them from the Enemy and to stop them being a wasted valuable resource to the purposes of God.

Through the Decade of Evangelism and Challenge 2000 which I am particularly committed to, we are encouraging evangelism and church-planting in every group of 1,000 people in every village, town and city of England. The purpose is to generate love instead of fear, light instead of darkness, hope instead of hopelessness. The life and power of God free us from fear, sin and the devil. His word and Spirit cause our energies to be redirected to bless the oppressed and those subject to social injustice.

We are not only free from sin for ourselves but free to bless others with the blessing with which we have been blessed. If every seat in our churches in the UK were taken on a Sunday, they would still only accommodate less than twenty per cent of the entire population. Hopeless!

While certain sections of historic Christianity are looking and sounding like clapped-out relics of previous centuries, hobbling around on their zimmer frames, disappearing into oblivion, we must create a radical alternative. We are not building ecclesiastical utopias. We don't have to pretend we are sinless. But we can declare that we are free from the continual, ongoing grip and possessive nature of the powers of darkness. What a gospel!

Stories and theology

Jesus often told stories to make a theological point. My stories of the innocent arrested in Tooting, the disbelieving Anglican professor and Linda's deliverance all point to dark forces at work resulting in a breakdown of relationships, mental fragility and emotional instability. Because the devil is not omnipresent (everywhere), demons (fallen angels) serve him in his proud godless purposes. Just as angels are ministering spirits serving heaven, so demons are sent to trouble those who wish to be like Jesus and then to enslave those who appear to be without hope and without God. Demonic forces take advantage of us in tiredness and weakness, in sickness and loneliness; that is in their very nature.

The devil and his demons are hostile to God and those who bear the image of God. In the Gospels there are several references to people being possessed by demons and there were a variety of effects, including dumbness

(Lk 11:14), epilepsy (Mk 9:17), public nakedness by choice and living in a cemetery (Lk 8:27).

Scripture also clearly distinguishes between people who are simply sick and others possessed by demons. Matthew wrote about 'those who were sick, suffering from all kinds of diseases and disorders, people with demons and epileptics, and paralytics — and Jesus healed them all' (Mt 4:24). Jesus often healed the sick without casting out demons. Then again, demons were cast out of people when there were apparently no signs of sickness. The two should not be confused.

Christ, the kingdom and darkness

Paul, in the Ephesian letter, called the devil and the demons 'powers of darkness'. Christ refers to himself as 'the light of the world' (Jn 8:12). The apostle Paul writes about 'the light of the glorious gospel of Christ' (2 Cor 4:4–6). On one occasion Christ turned to his disciples and told them that they were the light of the world (Mt 5:14) and Paul echoed this in his letter to the Ephesian Christians when he explained that they were 'children of light' (Eph 5:8).

So the world, the flesh and the devil are opposed to seeing the kingdom come now. They are opposed to seeing the kingdom come at all!

The answer to worldliness? Talking things out with God, worshipping and praising him on our own and with others. Most importantly, exposure to Scripture. The truth of Scripture sets us free from the illusions, fantasies and myths of the world.

The answer to fleshly inclinations, which lead us away from Christ and his purpose for our lives? Well, first to recognise what are the works of the flesh, the deeds of the flesh and those things which declare a lack of respect for God, ourselves, our friends, our enemies and the world around us. We need to be asking all the time, will this deed or action help us to be what God wants us to be and of course what we therefore want to be? We need to confront the sins of the flesh. The evil thought need not become evil thinking, the evil feeling need not become evil acting — but those thoughts and feelings need to be confronted with the truth.

And what of the devil? Scripture is clear. 'Submit yourselves therefore to God. Resist the devil and he will flee from you' (Jas 4:7). When we know we are under attack, we need to stand against the powers of darkness in prayer, boldly declaring who we are in Christ, what his plans are for our life and that we are not going to be seduced by the powers of darkness.

Spirituality has to do with allowing God's Spirit to help us make the right choices to see the kingdom come now! So what goes wrong with so many people who seem highly motivated to see God's kingdom come and his will done in our localities? Why does sin disqualify so many people, especially leaders? Why do the pull of the world, the lust of the flesh and demonic attack seem to go undetected — paralysing church communities?

I'll tell you a story.

5

Discovering the Kingdom — Together

On New Year's Eve 1990 my wife and I invited seventy friends to celebrate the past year and to dedicate ourselves to the coming decade. Close friends, national Christian leaders, neighbours, political and entertainment personalities laughed and chatted over food and wine, until Big Ben was about to strike.

I stood on the steps between two of our living-rooms, we raised our glasses 'to the King and the kingdom'. After the toast a few words were appropriate. 'Ladies and gentlemen, this is the decade we have waited for. This is a time I feel I have been born for. It is when we are going to see God move in great power particularly among the young, the movers and the shakers, and the entertainers of our nation.' Michael Green, the Anglican theologian and evangelist, spoke for us all, leading us in prayer as we offered ourselves to God for the nineties.

Since that time, the growing awareness of God's presence in many local churches, the development of evangelistic skills, church-planting initiatives and social action programmes, have only confirmed the sentiments of that special evening. Many of us have a sense that what took six years will take six months and what took six months will take six weeks. But in order for that to happen, we have to get things in order. When I was born again I was also born into a new family, but I was born badly. As a result of erroneous teaching, faulty theology and an inadequate pastoral system, health and maturity did not develop as swiftly as they could have done. For example, between the time I was born again and baptised in the Holy Spirit it was almost fifteen years! These days in our own church it is happening in fifteen minutes!

Pilgrim's progress

According to my own observation, the modern pilgrim's progress follows a fairly routine pattern. When responding to the gospel, the hearer is often overwhelmed with the knowledge of sin and separation from God. Having made a response, forgiveness and cleansing are experienced and the person is helped and counselled by those who know and love the Lord Jesus.

We will call our friend 'Lawson' (son of the law!). That person is quietly but firmly encouraged to join a Christ-centred congregation, pray regularly (perhaps every day and especially first thing in the morning), read the Scriptures daily and take the moral high ground.

Seven months go by before Lawson returns to his counsellor. While grateful for many changes in life, improved behaviour and a measure of fulfilment, defeat and failure are confessed. It is explained to Lawson that Jesus died for all of his sins, that he has two natures and that he will be a sinner to the day he dies!

He is now launched on a problematic course. On the one hand he is told to aim for perfection, but on the other that sin will dog him for the rest of his life. While struggling for perfection, his fate is sealed. If his confession is thorough he is bound to acknowledge sexual fantasy, dishonesty, maybe a little gossip and failing to speak up for others when he should. It is not difficult to imagine that a mild form of schizophrenia sets in.

But the pressure is on to fit into a religious system, to go with the party-line, dress in appropriate clothes (often hinted at rather than openly explained) and not hang around with the 'wrong sort'.

A false start

Next, Lawson has to gain membership of his local church. Water baptism or confirmation is necessary. (The latter may be performed by a bishop who is neither evangelical nor Bible-believing in any accepted sense of that phrase.) But neither can happen just yet, of course. After all, Lawson doesn't understand anything yet (not that one gets the impression that converts 2,000 years ago knew all that much about things either!). After some months, if not years, of learning and conforming, he is allowed baptism or confirmation, almost as a reward for good conduct, and welcomed into fellowship. In the New Testament they were baptised almost immediately, which led to 'newness of life' but in the twentieth century, newness of life must be demonstrated for some considerable time beforehand.

So instead of having the heart before the course, the cart is very much before the horse! A dangerous principle is forced upon Lawson, albeit from the sincere. Namely, prove yourself, do well, fit into the pattern of things and we will bless you.

Trying hard

Lawson has a go at 'quiet times' but occasionally or even regularly oversleeps! He feels a failure. However, he goes out witnessing regularly in the church team, often ending up embarrassed, tongue-tied or unhelpfully aggressive.

Not to be put off, he still has the highlight of the

week to come: the Lord's Supper, breaking bread or Communion. Sunday after Sunday, as a mental gymnast, he indulges in nothing short of mental idolatry. In the morgue-like stillness of the church he conjures up a mental image of the middle cross, the darkening sky and the mob at the foot of the cross. No one ever told him that he could express Jesus' death and triumphant resurrection in loud praise, a heavenly language, hands outstretched in the air, with tears, perhaps on his knees or prostrate before the Lord.

So he struggles beneath the law, having to feel something religious at a particular hour on the first day of the week. He tries to be thankful and genuinely is — but it is difficult to get good feelings at 10am in the morning when you have missed your breakfast. Occasionally he succeeds, producing a rosy warmth of pride, but normally he sinks into further condemnation because the emotional response hasn't happened.

Personally I challenge the validity of breaking bread or a Communion service, taken with loads of people whom you rarely talk to, who in some cases wouldn't even claim to know the Lord Jesus personally. It is absurd to be breaking bread together when the only 'communion' is between you and the Lord! The whole thing is a farce.

Jesus used satire and humour to communicate. Those of us in Christian public leadership should do the same. One of the great difficulties of being a communicator and a humorist is that whenever you try to be funny about something or somebody, you invariably find that Christian people did something even funnier than anything you could think up!

We are not wrangling about inessentials here. We are going to see thousands and thousands of young and older people born again, converted to Christ, and we have got to do better than Lawson. But it was hardly Lawson's fault.

Give it a rest!

A. W. Tozer noted that you could tell a lot from a church not only by what it said but by what it didn't say. And not only by what it said and didn't say but by what it implied in what it said and didn't say!

It is assumed Sunday is the Lord's day — without a shred of biblical evidence! Men shouldn't wear earrings — despite the fact that in the Old Testament, the men took their earrings off and threw them in the offering to rebuild the Temple! Jeans shouldn't be worn for worship or Bible teaching — despite the fact that worship is a life style and I am not aware of a biblical ban on denim! And so it goes on.

The current Keep Sunday Special Campaign is not based on the organisers' belief that Sunday is the Sabbath. Rather, with the breakdown of relationships, especially in the family, and our current culture of gathering on a Sunday for worship and teaching, working seven days a week will do several things. First of all, it is likely Sundays will be the second busiest trading day of the week. Secondly, and importantly for church leaders, many in the retail industry and ancillary commercial and industrial concerns will be obliged to work. Having once worked in the retail industry for ten years, I think it is complete balderdash to say that people will be free not to work on a Sunday if they wish!

But one's personal preference to maintain something within our culture is one thing; telling people they cannot sunbathe, swim, eat out in a restaurant or go to the cinema because it is the Lord's day is another.

The human body needs rest and one day of rest in seven is a good principle. That is not in question. But there is no divine statute to specify which of the seven. Many devoted church-goers are physically and mentally overworked on Sundays and — if they are part of the charismatic movement — emotionally overworked as well!

Very few non-charismatic congregations spend much time in worship anyway. They abound in preaching and prayer. Worship would barely clock up more than a few minutes and much of that would hardly rate as real worship by Old Testament standards, never mind New Testament ones. In the Old Testament songs were accompanied by a wide range of musical instruments (not just an organ or even a guitar). Songs were accompanied by dance, handclapping and shouts of joy, often interspersed with prostrations and awe-filled silences. That is not quite the same as the hymn-prayer sandwich or the endless singing of so-called 'new songs'.

Overcoming law and sin

One of the reasons I have spent so much time in the previous two chapters on the issues of legalism and sin is that both ensnare God's people, limiting their usefulness, causing them to live in the shadows rather than the bright light of the gospel.

Apart from my wife, who is my best friend, there are a number of friends around who know everything there is to know about me. There may be a few details I've not shared with them, but not by choice. What does that mean? It means, quite simply, I do not have to pretend any more! I can be myself in private and be myself in public. I don't have to be one thing in private and another in public. What a relief!

It is true that the church is only as strong as each member. Therefore personal holiness, purity, prayerfulness and integrity are vital — but we were never expected to go it alone.

Friends, friends, friends

While it is true that the church is only as strong as each member, legalists have little room for real friendship. Each

Christian is meant to have their own personal fellowship with God, narrow walk, quiet times, personal morality and decent behaviour. But such is the overemphasis on the relationship with those in heaven that there is little need of a relationship, an open friendship, with those on earth.

But friendships last for ever. If the friendships we are forming now are not going to count in the age to come, much of what we are doing in this time-space world is a complete waste of time. It is lunacy to imagine that we are not going to know anybody but Jesus in the age to come. We will not be walking around without identity, names or distinguishing features. Yes — we are going to know one another in the age to come. It will be different! It will be better!

God has given us to each other so that we can nourish, sustain, bless and influence each other. At times we need to correct and adjust each other, in an atmosphere of trust, appreciation and loyalty. We are not to possess people but to honour them, esteem them, enjoy and serve them in as many creative ways as we can find.

A relaxed evening among friends, when we can be ourselves, without any pretence, is a rich privilege — one that God intends. Sadly, many churches have a low-trust factor where members have almost to perform their Christianity rather than live it out in a relaxed fashion. How many friends do we have with whom we can truly be ourselves, without fear of being talked about or written about in groups that thrive on the stories of other people's failures?

Most of our church meetings and services are not designed for friendship and fellowship. They are designed to sit and listen to a speaker who is often high in a pulpit or on a platform. Of late, thank God, that has included extended times of worship, praise and adoration. But much of our church architecture is actually designed to hinder discussion, friendship and fellowship. Boxed-in pews, staring at the back of someone's head and fixed seating complete the task of ensuring we don't talk to each other during the 'sacred hours' of church.

But Jesus laid tremendous emphasis on friendship. 'No longer do I call you slaves . . . but I have called you friends' (Jn 15:15).

Business before pleasure?

Not only did Jesus have friends, he had a best friend, John. Peter and James were probably close runners-up! Scripture tells us that at one time Jesus had 500 disciples. Within that group he had seventy. Among the seventy were found to be twelve special followers. Among the twelve there seemed to be a special three and even within that three, there was what the Authorised Version of the Bible calls 'the other disciple, whom Jesus loved' (Jn 20:2). He seemed to favour John more than others on occasion, just as he favours some today more than others. People often say to me, 'Jesus hasn't got any favourites,' throwing their head back and shaking it in disgust. I normally reply, 'Well, you are probably saying that because you are not one of them!'

And who are our best friends? I don't have any close friends who dislike me, are continually correcting my every fault, gossip about me or seek to compete instead of co-operate. All of my close friends like me, believe in me and have an ongoing relationship involving a high degree of loyalty and trust. Of course, though we all have to say the hard things to each other at times, it is with reluctance and humility, not with an air of pride and superiority.

When we look at Jesus, we find that Scripture never records that he spent any time on his own with Judas. Yet many of us, particularly leaders, spend much of our time with the difficult, the unlovely, the time-consumers and sometimes the selfish. One of the reasons Christians in leadership look so tired, harassed and weary is because they spend so much of their time with people they do not like! True, the gospel encourages us to love the unlovely and give ourselves to those who are lonely, but not to the exclusion of developing carefree, enriching friendships.

Family and army

The nuclear family was not God's idea. Families in both the Old and New Testaments are always 'extended'. When Scripture mentions households, the reference is invariably to husband and wife, children and servants, in-laws and even senior administrators of household affairs.

It is no good expecting the Spirit of God to raise up an army with leadership, strategy and goals if our family life (and here again I mean not just the nuclear family model) is barely given any attention. A strong family life with leadership, purpose and goals will contribute to many families combining their energies to become the army of God. In the words of my friend, the singer/songwriter Dave Bilbrough, we are 'an army of ordinary people'.

But I do want to speak to many fellowships, particularly the so-called House Church/New Church variety that has sprung up over the last twenty years. Many of these independent churches and fellowships were founded on friendship. But their strength became their weakness. They want to hang on to past friendships, models of communication and rich times of being 'normal' to such a degree that it hinders them from swamping their area with prayer, gospel activity and ministry. If this friendship hurdle isn't jumped, God will have to raise up another company that will enable Christ to live in a body of believers to get his will done in that locality.

Friendship is not an end in itself. We have to ask what God wants to do with these friendships. The nature of all relationships changes. When I first became friends with Anona we had few responsibilities as we both lived at home with our parents. Then the nature of our relationship changed, as we not only shared a bed and a table but responsibilities of mortgage, garden and home. Then as our sons were born, the relationship changed again, as I had to give myself to work hard to not only pay the mortgage and general household bills, but to meet the expenses of a growing family. Anona had to give much of her time, affection and love to four in the family instead of just one.

So we cannot love everybody in the same way. God gives us the right to choose our friends to release us from a network of obligatory relationships. We are obliged to love. We are also free to choose!

Those of us in positions of responsibility among God's people can often get totally trapped with what the diary dictates and what the needs of others determine. We are all obliged to do things we are not best suited to and perform tasks for which we have few skills we can draw on. But it is important we understand that our ministry is what we enjoy doing, and that should be our main area of attention. The writer A. W. Tozer was called 'pastor'. He was everything but a pastor! Well aware of this fact, he rarely visited anybody in his large congregation in Chicago. But on one occasion he felt he ought to visit one of his elders who had been taken sick and was now hospitalised. As Tozer entered the ward, the elder spied him and was so shocked to see him doing a pastoral visit that he sat bolt upright in bed and uttered, 'I'm not that sick!'

Building relationships

I thank God for guiding me to share my life with others. I have been able to express my hopes and fears, dreams and nightmares, talk about things that cause me to raise my voice, stamp my foot, praise God, dance or cry. But how do we get from here to there? Well, I've noticed that most relationships tend to go through three stages.

Veneer

This is the stage where we are nicer than God himself. Even God is not as nice as most Christians. It is the highly polished stage.

The only way we can get to know each other is by the impression we leave with each other. Most of us like to impress, irrespective of whether or not we have the charisma, warmth and intellect that enables this. But if you are like me, we tend to give the impression that we are solid gloss and shine all the way through. There is of course nothing wrong with the initial veneer-type relationship. We operate on the veneer stage of relationships every time we visit our bank, collect our newspaper, eat a McDonald's or give a cheque to the milkman or postperson. The real sadness comes when we never get beyond that stage with people who know and love the Lord Jesus, with whom we have been praying, worshipping and fellowshipping for years.

The result is that we have what I call a 'carpet mentality'. All the nasty things get pushed under the carpet! In a local church we can become so aware of what is under the carpet that large protrusions cause us to walk around, in nimble-footed fashion, until we become experts at not talking to Mrs Brown about this, Mr Green about that and Mr Black about the other. But churches don't need carpets. While in the initial stages of a relationship, etiquette and grace may cause us to avoid issues, but in the long term, this sort of behaviour does not produce a high-trust factor.

When challenged about this sort of behaviour, we often reply, 'Well, I don't want to hurt so and so.' But I would suggest that if we really examine our motives, it is because *we* don't want to get hurt!

Disillusionment

The second stage of all relationships is disillusionment. For some it is almost total disillusionment, but for most of us it is partial disillusionment.

It is when we find out that Gerald Coates is not solid mahogany all the way through and that underneath is a substandard quality of material. Chip off the veneer by mentioning the wrong thing, behaving in an inappropriate way or by challenging one of his foibles — the veneer sheers off, all on its own, to reveal chipboard! We get disillusioned with one another because we have illusions about each other.

I am always being asked about well known friends of mine, either in politics, entertainment or in church leadership. Disillusioned people like to find flaws in others so that they can fellowship together in their disillusionment!

In the autumn of 1989 I was interviewed by Val Hennessy of *You* magazine, the colour supplement of the *Mail on Sunday*. It was meant to be a serious interview about Pioneer People — Cobham (then called the Cobham Christian Fellowship), my ministry with the Pioneer Team, the churches and the ministries we helped to initiate. Pioneer Trust has helped to staff and fund March for Jesus, Jubilee Campaign and ACET (AIDS Care, Education and Training). After Val Hennessy had come to one of our prayer-meetings attended by over 1,000 people drawn from around the locality, we lunched in Esher's Boulevard St Michel (the *Mail on Sunday* was paying!). Imagining that the article was about our Pioneer network of churches and ministries, I told her all about Danny Smith's hard work in the Jubilee Campaign for those suffering for their faith in various parts of the world. Of Dr Patrick Dixon's remarkable achievements with the AIDS initiative, giving unconditional care to dying AIDS patients irrespective of how they contracted the disease. Of our partnership with

Ichthus and YWAM; with March for Jesus and how hundreds of thousands had come out onto the streets to pray for the nation.

Perhaps I was naive, but Val Hennessy was not remotely interested in any of it. She had come to do an exposé on what she considered was a controversial evangelical church leader. Another writer quipped: 'Gerald Coates is neither a Flash Gordon, as some of his followers think, nor a Flash Harry, as his enemies would have us believe.' He continued, somewhat embarrassingly for me, 'Gerald Coates of Cobham has great flair and a predilection for hard work.' But Flash Harry is precisely what she thought I was and that was therefore how she was going to write, irrespective of the facts of the substance of our work.

'What is Cliff Richard's private life really like?' she enquired. 'Where does he live? What is his house worth and what do you think he is worth as a person?' My radar detected something so I refused to answer anything other than in bland general terms. What was she doing? She was looking for the inside story on someone far more famous than I will ever be and someone who to all intents and purposes looks flawless. Having made some investigations I now find that she is fairly disillusioned and cynical about life and people, as evidenced in so many of her articles.

So I say it again. We get disillusioned because we have illusions about people. We can look at individuals and imagine they haven't sinned for at least twelve months! We imagine they have never had an adulterous thought, or are unlikely to know what masturbation means. We assume they have hardly ever said a word out of place and have regularly acted with great dollops of wisdom and grace. This is of course fantastical nonsense!

Opt out or choose reality

Friendship has to get beyond the veneer stage. Even more than that, it has to get beyond the disillusionment stage, where the highly polished gloss is worn away in the daily round of communication, projects and close scrutiny.

But once through the veneer and disillusionment, we still have two options. The first is to opt out! We simply pick up another friendship, we fill the gap with someone else. Inevitably, we wear through the veneer and get disillusioned — it can take two or three weeks, two or three months or two or three years. In fact in some churches where people stay long enough (and most don't!) it is possible to have been in 'friendship and fellowship' with many people in the church with whom we are now merely on nodding acquaintance terms.

Why? Because having gone through the veneer and disillusionment stages we opted out and into another relationship. That is why we find it difficult to pray together, greet each other with warmth and reality and work together to see God's kingdom extended in our locality. But the other option is to enter the final stage through the rugged terrain of disappointments, weariness and the pain that loving people brings.

There is a legend about a traveller who was looking for the living God. Feeling he was nearing his destination, he enquired the way. The native pointed north across the barren terrain. 'That is where your living God lives,' he proclaimed boldly. Our pilgrim turned his head southwards and instantly saw a beautiful city, filled with colour, music and happy noises. 'What is that?' he enquired, pointing to his architectural discovery. 'Oh, that is God City,' replied the native. 'I thought you said God lived over there, across that rugged territory,' said the traveller. 'He does,' confirmed the native. 'Then why is that called God City?' our traveller asked inquisitively. 'Ah,' mused the native, somewhat embarrassed. He knew he would be disappointing his questioner. 'You see, those city-dwellers were also, like you, once travellers. They were looking for the living God as well. But when they discovered that he is found across that rugged, open plain, they decided to settle here, enjoying the distant presence of God, but in safety and without pain. They decided to build a city which they named after their God—though they never found him.'

The pain of reality

Conflict is the essence of drama. We are a part of God's unfolding drama across the globe. Conflict must therefore be expected. Superficial 'God City' is no alternative for those who are hungering and thirsting after reality. The apostle John explained that you cannot say you love God without loving your neighbour (1 Jn 4:20–21).

I would suggest that behind every so-called 'personality' or 'doctrinal' conflict, there is also an issue of righteousness and unrighteousness. That is also why we need to give attention to a life style that allows us to live in (a) work in (b) and worship in (c). Our neighbours never see us at work or worship. Those we work with do not see us at home or in worship and those whom we worship with never see how our Christian faith is extended to our neighbourhood or workplace.

The playboy philosophy of 'get what you can from the fellowship and when you have drained it dry, move on' has been adopted by far too many people. If the church gets too hot, drop it. If people dislike you, clear off. Never get too involved, never get hurt. Run your life the way you want it and simply use your friends to satisfy your needs. What a disgrace and what a tragedy.

A personal reflection

When Anona and I were married over twenty-five years ago, we exchanged rings. These were not only a token of our love, but also of an agreed commitment and exclusive attachment.

Eventually we hit a rough patch in the relationship. We wore through the various layers of veneer, including squeezing the toothpaste in the middle, leaving underwear on the floor and letting off wind at inappropriate times and in embarrassing venues. Unkind words damaged romance and prayer. Negative attitudes cast shadows over other bright areas of creativity and communication. We became disillusioned with each other!

At this stage, either party can allow stray emotional impulses to latch on to other people. We find emotional security and acceptance among others to the exclusion of our partner. But I had discovered some words of Dietrich Bonhoeffer who when writing to his niece shortly before his execution by the Nazis explained: 'It is not love that will keep your marriage alive, but marriage that will keep your love alive.' In other words, it is the commitment to the relationship (albeit with outside help and advice) that will keep loyalty and trust in harmony.

So having worn through the veneer stage, we were well and truly into the disillusionment stage. We went off for a weekend to the home of a friend who was abroad at the time. In our disillusionment we purchased a couple of inexpensive rings and, seven years after our initial commitment, we reaffirmed our covenant and our agreement to be faithful to each other. That exchange of rings, couched in affection, truth and kingdom purpose took our marriage on in leaps and bounds.

Committing ourselves to others merely for the purpose of convenience and gratification will be seen for what it really is. But an agreement-keeping God, a covenant-keeping God, can only be seen clearly among an agreement-keeping, covenant-keeping people. It is here that our actions speak louder than our words.

So in the age to come we shall know one another. The friendships we have now will be of worth and value then.

Scaffolding or building

Commitment to marriage, church buildings, programmes, the order of service and our unwritten liturgies, special conferences, tapes and books, Bible studies and the like is important scaffolding that helps us to build our lives into God and one another.

Scaffolding is used in order to get something built. The tragedy occurs when people become convinced that the scaffolding is the building! If you take away clergy and buildings, Sunday schools and conferences, choirs and social events — what is left? In many localities, precious little. But all of those things, while important, are the scaffolding to help us build our lives into God and into one another. We are living stones being built together as a body (Paul often mixed up his metaphors!).

But today we have gold-plated scaffolding, ecclesiastical classical scaffolding, new radical scaffolding, multi-coloured scaffolding with new materials! But it is all scaffolding. A builder, having heard me speak on this subject, explained that in the trade, scaffolding is simply called 'temporary works'. Our problem is we have made them permanent. To my mind, if we are going to see the kingdom come — now — everything is open to change except for the truth and the value we put on relationships. Even they change to accommodate God's purposes among us.

Moving on

For some of my readers this is a time of new beginnings — a time to move on — a fresh start. For others it will be a time of new beginnings for family and friends. Whatever you do, don't commit yourself and your finance to a church which tolerates sin, or positively encourages legalism. Don't support churches that put tradition above Scripture, which look down upon pioneers because they would rather be settlers. Don't do it. The sooner that sort of Christianity collapses the better.

Good churches do exist; thank God are existing and increasing in number. Some are found within denominational structures. Others are found outside of denominational church structures. Here there is a flexible leadership, birthed with kingdom vision, kingdom-now concepts including the issues of law and grace, the nature of sin and the positive ministry to help us overcome the world, the flesh and the devil. In such churches there is a strong emphasis on friendship. If you cannot create and lead such a church, it is vital that you seek to become a part of one — for your sake and for your children's sake.

I am amazed that adults will put up with wishy-washy liberalism, boring meetings and services, and teaching that contradicts Scripture. Most of these churches discourage member participation other than through official channels. Some twenty or thirty years on, many people are waking up to the fact that they have wasted the better part of their lives and in so doing have turned their children away from Christ and his church for ever. What a tragedy. And all because of the fond notion that God is going to renew a church whose leadership don't believe in the authority of Scripture, who have resisted the Holy Spirit and who are overseen by area-wide leaders who are all things to all men — but without the last bit: 'to save some'.

For God's sake, make the move, have a family conference; if you're single, a friendship conference. Invest your friendship into a group which has similar values to your own. We are not building ecclesiastical utopias. No church is perfect, and you joining it won't make it any more perfect! Nevertheless you have valuable skills to contribute, whatever your age, background or experience. Your money should be financing ministries which extend the kingdom instead of upholding the sort of Christianity which has caused the people of our nation to vote with their feet.

Find your friends, pray with your friends, plan with your friends and give each other the grace to take whichever course you wish; and remember — friendship lasts for ever.

6
A Prophetic Kingdom

Nothing brings the distant God into the here and now as does the prophet. Prophetic words and acts disturb, but are usually resisted by the religious, and are therefore seen as controversial. But just because a thing is controversial it does not make it prophetic! Over the last two decades, many in the body of Christ have come to terms with the phrase 'prophetic'. We have prophetic teachers, prophetic worship, prophetic dancers, and prophetic ministries engaged in social action. But what does the word 'prophetic' mean?

Prophetic roots

The word was first used in the Old Testament to describe the message of those who spoke to the people of Israel under what was claimed to be the inspiration of the Spirit of God. The prophet would often introduce his message (it was nearly always a man) with 'This is what the Lord says.' Commandments, promises of deliverance (either in the here and now or distant future), words of judgement, condemnation and even songs of praise would all come from such men. Most of us baptise hard sayings with soft names. The prophets failed to do this, with spectacular results!

Some of these prophecies were written down, either by the orator or by others and later edited to convey a total message. The important thing about prophetic ministry is that the prophet is aware that he or she speaks as God's mouthpiece and conveys what has been called 'foretelling' as well as 'forthtelling'. It will also be helpful to establish now that the ultimate test of prophecy was not only the outcome of, say, a prediction, but also faithfulness and loyalty to the message given through Moses (read Deuteronomy 13).

The Scriptures are not at all clear about the nature of prophetic inspiration. It is clear that most prophets were 'personally aware of a mighty, divine influence, which came over them and gave the words that they used the ultimate authority of a message from God himself'. So said Paul King Jewett, who was formerly Professor of Systematic Theology at Fuller Theological Seminary in Pasadena, California.

The word and words

Spoken words — as against written words — were the primary form of communication for prophets and prophecy. But they often embodied their message in symbolic acts. God knows that words aren't enough. Isaiah conducted part of his ministry without clothes or footwear (Is 20:2–6); Jeremiah shattered a clay pot (Jer 19); Ezekiel actually dug his way through a wall (Ezek 12:1–16); John the Baptist preached out in the desert, 'a voice crying in the wilderness', wearing strange clothes and eating health food!

By way of contrast, by the time we get to the New Testament there is a sense in which every Christian is a prophet since the Spirit of Christ has come upon all flesh and 'they shall prophesy'. But there did seem to be a special group who were recognised as prophets and who worked alongside apostles. Paul gave a very high rating to the gift of prophecy to edify, encourage and comfort the church (1 Cor 14:13).

It *appears* that prophetic ministry is often given impulsively or spontaneously, but some of the prophets carried their messages around with them for years. Perhaps these would be among the more mature, whereas the 'sudden impulse' type of ministry would be no less relevant but perhaps more localised than the mature. The prophetic ministry highlights truth in a way that cannot be achieved by reason alone, as with Bible teachers whose concern is proper exegesis and a fair and strict approach that is true to the text.

It has been claimed that when the first wave of apostles died out, without many obvious successors, those with the gift of prophecy also faded off the scene. Teachers were left in abundance. But the core of prophetic ministry concerns itself with ethical and social concerns. These show the unredeemed what it is like to live under the rule of the living God. This ministry was not confined to rational propositions and moral idealism!

Prophecy and the nation

Back in the Old Testament, prophets were often found bringing God's message to kings and playing an active role in national affairs. Perhaps Moses was the prototype who on one occasion was even called 'king' (Deut 33:5). The first two kings of Israel were also called prophets but later on the anointed king and the anointed prophet seemed to be the norm.

Leaping forward to the early church, we find the gift of prophecy at work throughout her new beginnings. But through the thirty years the Acts of the Apostles covers, there are only two predictive prophecies, interestingly both given by the same man, Agabus. One concerned a famine and how the church should be prepared for it (Acts 11:28) and the other prophesied Paul's end and Agabus used his girdle for prophetic symbolism. So prophecy is not mainly prediction and it could be argued that this type of prophecy is usually only given to seasoned, experienced prophets.

What's in a title?

However sexist it may sound today, 'man of God' aptly describes how they appeared to their listeners (Deut 33:1). God himself often described his prophets as his servants. Another word for a prophet was of course 'seer' which translated simply means 'one who sees'. We should not therefore be surprised that their seeing often came through dreams and vision.

Theologians explain that there are at least eighteen passages which associate prophetic inspiration with the activity of the Holy Spirit. These include the issue of prophetic ecstasy (Num 11:29; 1 Sam 10:6,10; 1 Sam 19:20,23). However, Jeremiah never mentions the Spirit of God in any context whatever throughout his entire ministry!

A major controversy

Given the fact that Scripture provides us with information describing the lack of the prophetic gift at various times of history, we have nevertheless to ask whether the prophetic message is the word of God in the same way that Scripture is the word of God.

Clearly, there were many prophecies given by recognised prophets and prophetesses which never found their way into Scripture, as for example those of the four daughters of Philip (Acts 21:9). We are not given any hint as to the quality and content of their prophetic utterances. Were they less true or relevant than others? So how did the early church accept or believe these prophetic utterances? For surely this will be a clue as to how we should treat prophetic ministry today.

The fact is that once prophetic ministry has been given, weighed by other prophetic ministries (local or national leaders) and there is a sense it is of God, it is difficult to treat it in any other way than as the word of the Lord. We do not treat Scripture in the special way we do because it is simply in a magic book, or with a sort of 'well, it's in the Bible so it must be true' sort of attitude. That is an appalling way to treat the truth! It is not that things are in the Bible and therefore must be true — rather, these things are true and that is why they are in the Bible!

For example, sitting in the home of the now Minister of State to the President's Office and Chief of Security for Uganda, I received a vision of a coup about to take place. Such a thing had not happened in Kampala for years, and though there was still fighting in the north of Uganda, it was sporadic. One could walk around the city of Kampala at 9 or 10pm at night without fear of being accosted by a beggar, never mind being attacked. Children played in the streets without fear of abuse or kidnap — unlike many Western cities I know so well!

I shared my observations with, I confess, great respect and caution, with this Christian man. Several weeks later, 600 armed troops stormed those buildings — but Dr Balaki Kyria and his armed forces were ready for them. I have heard that this, among other things, was a contributory factor to the President recommitting his life to Christianity, having seen his wife come to faith and his daughter healed. He is seeking to encourage Christian principles within the Cabinet, the armed forces and the police, dealing with the abuse of power. This has resulted in sackings and imprisonment for those who have taken advantage of people in illegal and corrupt ways. In December 1991, President Musevini hosted a national prayer breakfast. He was kind and courteous enough to send me a handwritten invitation.

However, in both the Old and New Testaments and in contemporary history, it is clear that people were unsure how to relate to the prophet. Prophets seem to possess the remarkable certainty of the lunatic or those who are privy to the counsel of God. Most, it seems, were completely unaware of the existence of voices other than their own.

The prophets were invariably creative thinkers and some might even say actors. What some might regard as a visual aid empowered the message even further. The prophet Elisha introduces King Joash to symbolic but prophetic action when the arrow of the Lord's victory is shot against Syria. Elisha then asks how far the king has faith to take hold of this enacted word of promise. His response (found in 2 Kings 13:14) determines future events.

A mine-field?

New as the prophetic ministry is to God's people in these latter years of the twentieth century, it will be helpful to distinguish between prophetic people who get it wrong and false prophets. The essence of the false prophet is that he or she calls the people of God to follow after other gods and instigates rebellion against the Lord (Deut 13:2–10). The true prophet endeavours to stem the tide of wrong-doing and call people back to holiness and a personal relationship with God. There is therefore an appropriate message of judgement upon sin.

It must also be said that while the message of the false prophet is often one of peace (without going to the root of the breakdown of personal and corporate morality), that is not to say that the genuine prophet from God may not on occasion have a message of peace. Peace comes when we cease to resist God's will for our lives. But peace can only come when we are making heaven happy through an act and a life of repentance. C. S. Lewis commented that repentance isn't something we have to do before God will have us back; repentance simply describes the route back. Shallow optimism marks a false prophet. His prophecies are without moral content, which injures and is designed to hurt those who are faithful to God.

Testing prophets and prophecy

There are two main abuses of prophecy. The first is performance-driven: what can only be described as ecstatic frenzy, loud shouting and, by the close of the 'prophetic word', a face that makes a beetroot look as though it needs a blood transfusion! However, the apostle Paul makes it quite clear that 'the spirits of the prophets are subject to the prophets'. We are to be in full possession of our faculties, to the degree whereby we actually choose to speak or not to speak and don't end up blaming God for making us do things. He is not a manipulator, threatener or cajoler. He may impress things upon us, reveal things to us, but we at all times must remain in possession of our faculties (1 Cor 14:32–33).

The second abuse comes from a 'lone ranger' style of ministry. Scripture encourages us never to give prophetic ministry or prophets undiscerning reverence. A couple of tests were applied to anything that claimed to be prophetic. The first was quite simply to 'let the others discern' (1 Cor 14:29). There may be some difference of opinion as to whether the 'others' are prophets, the church as a whole or the leadership of the church. But the fact is, no one is allowed to prophesy in a local church situation without prophetic ministry or the church — with the elders or leaders — weighing the message and the spirit in which it is given. Everything we say and do is to serve. If it does not serve God's purpose and violates God's anointed leadership it must be rejected, otherwise it will cause chaos.

Of course, if the leaders and the church are allowing promiscuity, outright lying, gross heresy — all of which are clearly condemned in Scripture — that is a different story. But I am writing to charismatic evangelical churches where there may well be differences over a wide range of issues — but that is different. These are neither moral nor doctrinal issues.

Apostolic/extra-local ministry, in partnership with the local leadership, is another added check here. Strong manipulative voices may threaten leadership and sway a church but with objective, extra-local ministry, regularly involved and their seniority and experience recognised, spurious things are less likely to happen. Independent lone-ranger churches, however, must not be surprised if they give birth to independent lone-ranger ministries!

One of the reasons why there continue to be difficulties within charismatic churches is that the one-man ministry has given way to the every-man (or -woman) ministry! Everyone has something to say, and say it they do! There are no checks or balances, and no bed or banks for the river to flow along. Everyone does what is right in their own eyes. Paul clearly teaches and reason dictates that this is an unwise, unhealthy and unhelpful course to take. Leadership must be given and honoured.

The second test of a prophecy is whether it is in line with Scripture. The test of the true prophet, or indeed any mature Christian, is that the person has acknowledged that 'the things which I write to you are the Lord's commandment' (1 Cor 14:37). This clearly indicates that the prophetic ministry was not the primary source of truth, or even new truth, to the church, but that apostolic ministry was. Therefore those who exercised apostolic ministry were greatly concerned about any prophetic insight which removed the foundation they had laid, or violated Scripture.

The Old Testament prophet ministered in a subordinate role to Moses who provided the moral and doctrinal framework in which the people of God operated. The New Testament prophet operated in submission to apostolic ministry.

I am deeply disturbed by both speakers and writers who are not accountable to a local church. Prophetic ministry and leadership are often virtually unrelated to any national or international prophetic forum that can weigh their ministry. Many speakers and writers have an uncanny ability to tell the church what to believe and how to conduct themselves while failing in a spectacular fashion even to attend a local church themselves! They refuse to make themselves realistically accountable to any peer group. I have found that many national/international prophetic ministries relate to absolutely nobody! They have an 'I have heard from the Lord' syndrome. Or they surround themselves with little people who may well have wisdom and even a good teaching ability — but are about as prophetic as the proverbial plank.

The women also?

My traditional upbringing among God's people told me that women should be 'silent in church'. That seemed quite straightforward to me. However, there were anomalies. They were not allowed to preach publicly, particularly in front of men. We didn't believe in prophecy in the Brethren, from men or women, so that never came into the equation. Women were not allowed to pray publicly in front of men. But they were allowed to sing publicly! Not only corporately and publicly but often as a solo! Praise and worship, whether it be with the old hymn or recently written song, is only prayer put to music. So it began to seem rather odd to me.

Over twenty years later there has been a lot more research done on the subject of women in leadership and ministry. For an in-depth treatment along with biblical exegesis, Pioneer's publishing arm — Pioneer Direct — has published an excellent book entitled *Women in Leadership and Ministry* by Martin Scott. This Word UK/ Pioneer imprint is believed to be one of the best on the subject. But without going into lengthy detail, there is sufficient evidence in Scripture, in both the Old and New Testaments, to see that the word 'prophet' is used of both men and women.

For example, there was Miriam, the sister of Moses (Ex 15:20); Deborah, who was married to Lappidoth (Judg 5:7; 4:4); Huldah, who was married to the keeper of the royal wardrobe (2 Kings 22:14); Noadiah, who with others formed the alliance against Nehemiah (Neh 6:14) and Anna, who on seeing the child Jesus broke into praise and adoration (Lk 2:36). There were also Philip's four daughters, in Caesarea, who prophesied (Acts 21:9). Clearly, there was prophetic ministry around which, though recognised, did not appear in the canon of Scripture but was known to apostles such as Dr Luke who wrote what we call the Acts of the Apostles.

The apostle Paul himself, in line with the teaching and indeed prediction of Joel, makes it clear that prophecy was developed and exercised by people irrespective of their gender (1 Cor 11:4–5). Of course, wherever there is an original there is always a fraudulent copy, generally called false prophecy in the Scriptures. Jezebel (Rev 2:20) is a classic and well-known case.

Words are not enough

God knows that words are important. He is committed to his word and has expressed himself through words. But the writer to the Hebrew believers explained that although in the past God had spoken in 'bits and pieces', in these last days he has spoken to us 'through his Son'. Everything else pointed to Jesus Christ — types, shadows and forms all point to him.

Just as we look back to Calvary to find redemption and in that redemption forgiveness, cleansing and the gift of eternal life — so those in Old Testament times looked forward in faith to that day. Apart from the importance of Scripture we also have the concrete historic facts of Christ's birth, life, death and resurrection. The Old Testament believers looked forward without any of that concrete evidence. They had to be even more convinced and convicted that God's will was in his word and therefore the promise is as valuable as the fulfilment — because of him who gave the word.

But God knows that words are not enough. That is why the prophets often dramatised their messages. These were not little dramas and skits, put on to liven up uninteresting meetings or boring services; most were conducted outside of that sort of forum anyway.

For example, there was confusion in the New Testament church about the roles of Scripture and prophecy, particularly when extremely charismatic personalities emerged on the scene. So later the apostle Paul had to underline the difference between Judaism with its written law (Torah) and Jesus who was, and still is, the living Word. The 'letter' represents law and the 'Spirit' the very life of God.

However, the Spirit in Scripture is almost always connected with oral communication. 'Men moved by the Holy Spirit spoke from God' (2 Pet 1:21). (We have already established that 'men' must also have included women in the light of the above paragraphs.) 'Letter' is almost always connected to the gift of writing. The word 'letter' in Greek is *gramma*, which shares the same root as the Greek for 'handwriting'. Paul writes: 'Now, however, we are free from the law, because we died to that which once held us prisoners. No longer do we serve in the *old way of a written law* but in a *new way of the Spirit*' (Rom 7:6 GNB; italics mine).

Elsewhere he gratefully declares:

> You yourselves are the letter we have, written on our hearts for everyone to know and read. It is clear that Christ himself wrote this letter and sent it by us. It is written, not with ink but with the Spirit of the living God, and not on stone tablets but on human hearts. We say this because we have confidence in God through Christ. There is nothing in us that allows us to claim that we are capable of doing this work. The capacity we have comes from God; it is he who made us capable of serving the new covenant which consists not of *a written law but of the Spirit. The written law brings death but the Spirit gives life* (2 Cor 3:2–6 GNB; italics mine).

Writing is a superb means if you wish to convey precise and accurate information. It is ideal if you want to refer to material for analysis. I write around 3,000 letters a year and consequently I can be quoted on a number of issues. However, there is a drawback!

Several times people have received communication from my office and asked, 'What did he mean by this line?' Or, 'This surely needed some qualification!' They might ask, 'Did Gerald write this with a smile or through clenched teeth?' Certainly I have to confess to being woefully guilty of communicating in writing things which should have been said to someone either on the telephone or face to face. Then they can detect the tone of my heart, the qualifying sentiments and the pastoral concern for the other person. As the old adage states, written words objectify — spoken words personify.

The limitation of writing is simple. It lacks the creative breadth and charisma which is at the core of all good communication. My autobiography *An Intelligent Fire*, published in the spring of 1991, virtually sold out within the first twelve months. I had hundreds of letters from people in various parts of the world, many of which said 'I could almost hear you speaking when I read your autobiography.' I admit I have been somewhat pleased by these comments; they are infinitely better than 'I could hear someone else speaking as I read your book!'

However, if writing, despite its obvious merits, has limitations, so does spoken communication.

I'll say it again

Communication through speech has with it the ever present tendency to change facts in order to convey a suitable impression. So certain points of a story are highlighted, promoted and enlarged to grab the attention of listeners and make an indelible mark on both heart and mind. Francis Young says:

> The good story-teller highlights the important event and often completely disregards what he (or she) regards to be side issues. The better the story-teller, the more this is so! The good story-teller extracts and to some extent distorts, in order to bring about the proper sequence of events.

Stories belong to religion. If you draw up a philosophy or a system of doctrine, you have to avoid contradiction and be coherent. But when talking about God, the subject is too big to pin down. For example, are we saved by faith or works? Did Jesus reconcile an angry God to humanity or a hostile creation to God? Both contain part of the truth, but such an approach is incapable of embracing the whole paradox. We are attempting to speak of matters which are beyond human comprehension; too full of depths, questions and doubts. Stories strike a deeper chord.

Oral communication is therefore a better means of conveying the spirit of an issue, though it may not be the best medium for conveying accurate details. Spoken words generate life and draw all their power and strength from tone, texture and sound. Speakers and speaking convey presence. Spoken words should be full to the brim with life, shape, and richness and are of quite a different order from the written word.

A thin line?

The God of heaven wrote hardly anything at all. There were of course the two tablets upon which were written the Ten Commandments. He scribbled words of judgement on a palace wall. But that is it! It is not recorded that Jesus wrote anything which we in the twentieth century could benefit from today. He scribbled in the dust, but whether it was a cartoon or the Ten Commandments we are not given a clue.

While the religious people handed out advice based on text and written information, Jesus knew the kingdom of God was beyond written definition. He did of course honour what was written, he read it, studied it and absorbed it as well as taught it. But often he would ask, 'Unto what shall I liken the kingdom of God?'

Scripture never argues the case of prophets; it assumes their presence in any local church. But while the Book of Revelation is the only book in the New Testament which is given over almost entirely to prophecy, John, the author, never refers to himself as a prophet! It is he who nevertheless gives us this insight: 'The testimony of Jesus is the spirit of prophecy' (Rev 19:10). William Barclay said of this verse that 'it is an ambiguous phrase and a very important one'. But whichever commentary you read and whatever interpretation is put on that statement, there is an undeniable relationship between prophecy and all that Jesus has done and is doing today by his Spirit.

We should not therefore be surprised when although

God is committed to his word and words, the prophets dramatise their prophetic ministry. We in the Protestant church (reacting against Roman Catholicism with its idols, stained-glass windows, ceremonial dress and artistry) have relegated the arts, including drama, to the world. And we should not be surprised that the world has filled them up with what only the world could fill them up with. Whatever it is, it is rarely either Christ's word or his Spirit.

But we also need to understand that a respectable church will never turn this nation round for God. So the prophets are not always respectable people. Micah stripped off and went naked to enforce how God saw Israel's shame and spiritual nakedness; Isaiah himself went about naked for three years (Is 20:3) as a sign of impending judgement:

> The emperor of Assyria will lead away naked the prisoners he captures from those two countries. Young and old, they will walk barefoot and naked, with their buttocks exposed, bringing shame on Egypt. Those who have put their trust in Sudan and have boasted about Egypt will be disillusioned, their hopes shattered (Is 20:4–5 GNB).

Jeremiah purchased a waistband, put it on and then went and hid it. His message for Israel was formed from that apparently odd event (Jer 13:1–11). Later he was instructed to go and buy a pot and gather leaders and then smash it in front of them to illustrate the prophecy. Hosea married a prostitute; Jeremiah was forbidden to marry; while Ezekiel was forbidden to mourn. All this was to bring God's feelings and thoughts into individual lives and society as a whole. Rational men and women are not expected to behave like that. But although God is rational and the gospel is rational, the gospel is not simply full of rational propositions and moral idealism. God has got feelings too. He laughs and cries, he is angry and jealous.

Sometimes it takes a prophet to see the irony of a Howard Hughes, reputedly one of the world's richest men, dying of malnutrition. It takes a prophet to see that the West is poised between the raised fist (megalomania/force) and the raised phallus (eroticism/sensuality). It takes a prophet to see 'through the eye' rather than simply 'with the eye' as Blake put it.

Working it out

One important thing to remember with all prophecy is that most of the prophets, in both the Old and New Testaments, were not at all sure what they were prophesying about, never mind how it would be fulfilled. Few actually believed that a virgin would conceive and give birth to a son. Few lived with the daily conscious understanding of a suffering Messiah — otherwise they wouldn't have crucified him. Even in the early days of the church, there was virtually no understanding of salvation being for the Gentiles as well as the Jews, until after the incident with Cornelius and his household, all having been wonderfully baptised in the Holy Spirit.

Scripture teaches that most prophecy is to 'edify, exhort and comfort'. The EEC will help you remember that! Of course it can be corrective, directive and predictive, but that is not the norm. There were also things prophesied which, in the lifetime of the prophet, never came to pass. Joel, prophesying about the Day of Pentecost, is a well-known case.

The issue of false prophets and prophecy in Deuteronomy does not deal with errancy but idolatry. Sometimes what the prophet said didn't apparently come to pass. Jonah prophesied, but through prayer and intercession God's heart was changed. But Jonah never got stoned! He was grateful for that; he did not want to go to Nineveh in the first place! No, the judgement of death on the prophet is not only given for words that do not come to pass, for there are several interpretations of what could have happened or might yet happen. A false prophet is one who leads God's people into open rebellion and idolatry. Rebellion against God and his word and, as often is not the case, his people.

I would suggest that almost all prophecy is conditional, if not all. God has given us ability to choose life or death, to serve him or ourselves, to humble ourselves or to strut around in religious arrogance. But if giving prophecies demands humility, receiving them demands the same humility.

It's becoming clearer

After I had written my autobiography *An Intelligent Fire* I had to ask Kingsway, the publishers, for the manuscript to be returned. New events were being fulfilled before our very eyes, as a result of two significant prophecies. In the closing chapter, *New Directions*, I explained the nature and content of the prophecy that the controversial Paul Cain gave me in front of 1,000 leaders.

Without knowing who I was, or having met me, he spoke about God helping me through every controversy. He said that I was not in the geographic will of God. That this had to do with our church gathering centre, rather than where I was living. He spoke of an old metal building which he didn't understand. Confidentially we were negotiating for a large metal aircraft hangar not far from Cobham, though the Pioneer People — Cobham had met for twenty years in the centre of the town. The aircraft hangar is in another area and was a big challenge to our understanding of local church. He concluded that he saw five people in our family, and that he saw 'Jo, Nathan and Jonathan'. He said that one looked 'about thirteen, slim with fair hair' and went on to say that he 'somehow looked older'. Meeting afterwards quite by accident, he gave me a card on which he had written this prophecy. It included many things that he had not made public such as 'crowds marching' — a clear reference to March for Jesus — and the fact that the black metal warehouse was surrounded by vegetation — something that nobody could have possibly known other than three or four local leaders.

Jonathan is our youngest son, who at the time was slim, had fair hair and was coming up to his thirteenth birthday. We call him Jo, everybody does. However, Nathan is a lad who had been given to me by another family in the church to train him up in ministry and to prepare him for a working relationship with Pioneer. He is slim, has fair hair and was sixteen! But underneath 'Nathan' Paul Cain had written 'adopted ???' We obviously put 'Nathan' and 'adopted' together, although we have not officially adopted him. Rather, I have taken him under my care. But he was clearly given to us by the family with no strings attached.

Then in October 1991, almost by accident, my wife found out just before her forty-fourth birthday that her 'parents' were not her parents; she was adopted! Through a series of quite remarkable phone calls she found out that her mother was still alive and is a born-again evangelical! This has opened up a wide range of doors for her to share her faith and her story with neighbours and friends and a number of movers and shakers. So what did 'adopted' refer to? Perhaps both of them?

So we need to approach prophecy with humility. We must not accept it all without exercising our critical faculties, or reject it all because we can't make cerebral sense of it. As someone has said, 'If you want to hear God laugh, tell him your plans.' Another added, 'If you want to hear him laugh even louder, tell him what you know.'

Prophetic direction

Scripture continually refers to 'this age' and 'the age to come'. It would appear that these two ages are separated by the Second Coming of Christ and all that surrounds that glorious event. While the kingdom of God ultimately belongs to the age to come, and will be realised only in that age, the transition from this age to that age does not happen in the twinkling of an eye. There is what can only be described as an overlapping of the two ages. If conservative evangelicals futurise the kingdom (almost everything then but very little now), charismatic evangelicals have by reaction brought everything into the here and now.

But if prophecy exhorts, edifies and comforts us now, it also points us to the future, gives us hope. This is true of both the prophetic writings of Scripture and good contemporary prophecy.

Satan has been defeated at Calvary, but we have a part to play in the here and now in ensuring that he is given as little ground as possible. Still, deluded as he is by pride, he seeks to blind the eyes of this world. But the kingdom of heaven came to the earth through Christ, and invaded the realm of Satan. Jesus did this in his life but primarily at Calvary. As salvation for all nations was in sight, Jesus cried, 'It is finished.' The job was done, forgiveness for all could be experienced.

So how central are the cross and the resurrection to the issue of the kingdom, the age in which we live and the age to come? Should we be seeking to change the world or to let it run down, hastening the coming of Christ?

Prophetic scriptures can help us here and give us clarity. First, they help us to avoid wasting time in trying to improve things which, in this age, cannot be improved — an error into which we might fall if we insist that the kingdom of God is all now and there is not much more to come. They also help us not to waste time by being inactive in areas where we *can* do something to bring about the transition from the 'now' to the 'then' — areas we might fail to recognise if we believe that the kingdom is almost entirely future and that little can be expected now. I suggest there has been a missing element in so much gospel preaching and living.

7

The Cross, the Resurrection and the Kingdom

So far in *Kingdom Now!* we have looked at the constitution of the kingdom, the emphasis of Jesus' ministry being his Father and the kingdom, and many of the scriptures drawn from Jesus' teaching on the nature and purpose of the kingdom.

We have looked at who the kingdom is for, and who found it through Jesus' teaching. We have been reminded that Jesus is the pioneer of our faith and how we all need to pioneer our way out of darkness into light, out of the cause of relational disharmony into reconciliation, out of churchianity into relationships and of the need to pioneer new methods of communication if we are to reach the lost.

We have also been reminded that although Jesus announced that the kingdom of heaven was 'at hand', just around the corner as it were, our eschatology (our view of end time things) helps us to do everything in the light of those eschatological goals — relational unity of the body of Christ (Jn 17) and the networking of our world with the gospel (Mt 24:14).

To release all of that, you need a kingdom which is full of grace rather than laws imposed externally. Grace in relationships and grace in the way we do things, providing they are within the broad teaching of Scripture. We have remembered how that grace keeps us from sin and keeps us open to a relationship with God even after we have sinned. We observed that temptation to act independently from God and violate his word and ways comes from the world system, fleshly instincts and the devil or the powers of darkness. Scripture gives us clear guidelines as to how to deal with those three areas of attack.

As we 'discovered the kingdom together' we saw the importance of friendship, the body of Christ, and the higher value of interdependency over independency and dependency.

Finally, we saw how this kingdom is a prophetic kingdom. The church is to be a prophetic statement and we need to rediscover and restore to the church prophetic teaching, signs and wonders, dreams and visions. As it was in the Old and New Testaments, so it can be in the latter years of the twentieth century. Heads of states and the histories of nations can be turned around by a prophetic word, a vision or a dream. We pray as though everything depends on God. We work, serve and discipline ourselves as though everything depends on us!

What now?

Some may therefore be a little bewildered that I have left the cross of Christ to this, the last chapter. But there is a reason for this.

Almost everybody reading *Kingdom Now!* is a Christian. Each one of us has responded to the gospel as we have heard it, seen it and experienced it. We have believed on Jesus, his birth, life, death and resurrection. We have understood, with a growing awareness, that without the cross there is no remission of sin (Heb 9:22). But in some strange way Jesus, upon that cross, became sin for us (2 Cor 5:21).

Jesus' death on the cross now makes it possible for us to be kingdom people, living under grace while walking in the ways of God. We can be free from the habitual binding nature of sin, seeking to be prophetic with words, works and wonders, building the sort of relationships in our villages, towns and cities that will cause the unbeliever to ask questions. Remember — nearly all evangelism in the New Testament took place in answering the questions.

The cross speaks of death, sacrifice, blood and gore. This place of untold suffering by the most innocent Man in the world has been somewhat sanitised by stained-glass windows, romanticised by the liberals and placed at the central point of Christianity by traditional believers. Herein lies our difficulty. Evangelical and liberal/traditional believers are, in their preaching, liturgy, church buildings and art forms, almost wholly occupied with the death of Christ.

When I went along to our local Anglican church on Good Friday, I could understand why people were looking so glum, singing sober things, and why they lowered their voices when they were reading the Gospel narratives about the crucifixion of Christ. My problem was it was no different on Easter Sunday! There was an odd spot of life in a hymn or two but I fancied that had more to do with the music than the people singing the songs!

Of course, if in order to meet with God's people one has to walk through a cemetery, sit in a building surrounded by plaques and memorials to the dead and stand on the tombs of those who have gone before, it is difficult to feel anything other than a little bit deathly. When loud voices, raw passion, swaying, clapping, raising hands and lusty singing are regarded as shallow emotionalism — the scene is set. The alternative is often called reverence, but it is often more likely to be something else! Death. Death. Death.

Of course, much church behaviour has little to do with

reverence. Scripture exhorts us to sing and dance, clap and shout. The Book of Psalms is an entire book in the Bible devoted to praise and worship with musical instruments. It gives us guidelines as to what is pleasing to God and what is not when it comes to praise. True, many charismatic groups should look at their liturgy instead of plodding from song to song with a similar beat, repetitive style with a complete absence of creativity. But better the signs of life than the signs of death.

The central theme

My contention is that the cross is not the central point of Christianity — the resurrection is!

Thousands of men died on crosses in Jesus' lifetime. None was as pure and innocent as he. None could do what he did. I have already underlined the fact that without the cross, without Jesus becoming a substitute for our crimes, there would be no gospel, there would be no forgiveness, no redemption, no reconciliation with God, no gift of eternal life. But the astounding note of triumph in the New Testament does not surround the cross — but rather the resurrection. The great theme of the New Testament is that Christ is alive!

The early Christians were not martyred for saying that Jesus had died for them. Such a notion would have been regarded as silly and odd by the unbelievers. No — men, women and children were butchered, torn limb from limb and set on fire at Nero's garden parties because they said that Jesus was alive. What is more, that he is King of all kings, President of all presidents, benevolent Dictator of all dictators, Prime Minister of all prime ministers. Authority doesn't like that!

James Gibbons wrote: 'We do not attach any intrinsic virtue to the cross; this would be simple and idolatrous. Our veneration is referred to him who died upon it.'

Yet Jesus in his ministry brought the God who was almighty and 'up there' into the intimacy of 'Abba', picturing a father with a child on his knee. He was at great pains to explain that God is not a hard taskmaster, but delights to answer prayer, enjoys being pestered, and gives good gifts to his children.

He had already spoken about sacrifice and his apostles were later to write about being a living sacrifice as against a dead one. About laying aside every weight and the sin that so easily besets us, so that we can get God's will done. But the central theme of the New Testament is that the Christ who died is now alive. That we are to live happy, holy and sacrificial lives in the power of the resurrection so that the humble of heart can find salvation.

More enemies

I appreciate that in stating that the resurrection is the central point of Christianity I shall gain few friends. But this is what Scripture teaches. However, there is nothing more uncertain of success than to try to introduce a new order of things. This is because the initiator will have as enemies those who have done well under the old order, and cautious defenders among those who may do well under the new one! But that must not deter us from speaking the truth.

The preoccupation with death in the church, its hymnology, preaching and emphasis is in sharp contrast to Jesus' offer of life. The remarkable thing is that the catacombs revealed paintings of fish, peacocks and biblical stories. Themes relating to Noah and his ark, Abraham and his ram and Daniel and the lions, along with Jonah and the whale, were all clearly visible. But there was no cross!

It was some 250 years later, after Scripture had been written and completed, that the cross was accepted as the symbol for the Christian faith. This can be a helpful visual aid as we remember the tremendous cost of our salvation. But the church has made an enormous mistake in hanging, standing, nailing, glueing and generally displaying crosses in every edifice that is remotely religious.

The Bible is remarkably low key about the cross of Christ. The writers certainly could not be accused of squeezing every bit of juice out of the story. It plainly states the simple facts of Jesus carrying a cross, the personalities involved, the crucifixion itself and the remarkable words that fell from our Lord's lips. Matters surrounding the cross are given but a sentence or two. There is no sensationalising here.

I sometimes feel, when listening to charismatic and non-charismatic evangelicals, that they could evoke a similar response from people who are listening to a story of a guilty man who was hung or electrocuted. With the average Sunday morning or evening congregation looking as though they are about to be shot, or have just taken a large overdose of Horlicks, what is needed is the Spirit of resurrection.

We rarely see tears of brokenness, or indeed little 'outward sign of inward grace'. Few kneel spontaneously, visibly or audibly rejoice in the reading of Scripture. This is the prevalent mood within the church. 'Its name is public opinion,' said Mark Twain. 'It is held with reverence, it has settled almost everything. Some think it is the voice of God.' And this is precisely what any individual will find themselves up against when they suggest that these Sunday morning capers have little to do with the Christ who is today risen, reigning and ruling.

Faith and work

One doesn't need faith to believe in Calvary. It is an historical fact, documented by believer and unbeliever alike. It is mentioned in the writings of unbelieving Jews. But we do need faith to believe in the resurrection, to worship the unseen, to be obedient to the invisible.

The kingdom of God is not a celestial utopia to be aimed at but an ever present reality to be lived in. The sharing of bread and wine in the context of a meal is sufficient for us to remember the humility of God, the cost that was paid and the need to develop and nurture a heart and mind of gratitude. But the 'ever present reality to be lived in' relates us to the world in which we live, how we confront its values, affect its thinking, and seek to be salt and light in society.

The kingdom of God is not merely an alternative to political injustices. William Temple was of course absolutely right when he said: 'There is no structural organisation of society which can bring about the coming of the kingdom of God on earth, since all systems can be perverted by the selfishness of man.'

The Spirit-filled, resurrection-centred church will find itself in direct conflict with the goals, ideals and values of the world in which it lives. We must not cry 'Behold, Calvinism is at hand' or 'Behold, the charismatic movement is at hand'; we must not even cry 'Behold, the evangelical church is at hand.' It is the kingdom which is at hand.

And when that kingdom comes through the holy lives of believers, the private sharing of the gospel and the public proclamation and preaching of the gospel; when the prophetic word lights a flame in the hearts and minds of individuals and people groups and signs and wonders are done, proving that the gospel is not simply a set of rational propositions and moral idealism — war is declared. Two groups claiming the same piece of territory are always engaged in war. The earth is the Lord's but it 'lies in the hands of the Evil One' (1 Jn 5:19).

If it is true that no religion has ever been greater than

its idea of God, then how we worship and the spirit of that worship is crucial. It is this issue of what God is like that has occupied the noblest minds.

Idolatry is the creation of a god who is no God. Or transforming God into somebody that he isn't. On one occasion God said to his people, 'You thought that I was just like you' (Ps 50:21). But God is altogether different. He is omnipotent (all-powerful). God has so much power that at the end of this age he will raise up, out of the graves, every human being who has ever lived (Jn 5:28–29). He has shared this power with individuals and with the corporate many-membered son, the body of Christ. His Spirit is given to help us live and love, pray and praise, serve and sacrifice and to see God's kingdom come and his will done on our part of the earth and beyond.

God acts without effort. He does not expend energy that must be replenished. There is a self-sufficiency that makes it unnecessary for him to look outside of himself to renew his strength. All the power he requires to do what he purposes rests in his infinite existence. Our God does not faint and neither does he grow weary (Is 40:28).

He only acts in ways that are consistent with his word and with his promises. He cannot lie, tolerate sin, save unrepentant wrongdoers or punish innocent people.

Created beings?

Perhaps somewhat humorously, the Lord asked where Job was when he, the Lord, was laying the foundations of the earth. 'Who laid its corner stone, when the morning stars sang together and all the sons of God shouted for joy?' (Job 38:4–7). There appears to be a clear reference to angels here, as the 'morning stars' are mentioned synonymously with 'sons of God'. Clearly this is not a reference to literal stars, since the universe had not yet been created. Scripture doesn't tell us when angels were created, in the creation order, so we can only assume they were created before time and space as we know it.

Yet at some point between their creation and the fledgling beginnings of humanity, something went terribly wrong. A significant group of angels rebelled against their Creator God (Rev 12:9). Angels are not robots. They have wills; we understand this as they chose to rebel against God. These angels are now known as demons. Christ refers to 'the devil and his angels' (Mt 25:41) and John refers to Satan as the great red dragon, whose 'tail drew the third part of the stars of heaven, and did cast them to the earth' (Rev 12:4). We have already seen that 'stars' refers to angels, so it appears that one third of the angelic realm rebelled against God and went with Satan.

It is not difficult to conclude that God and goodness have an Enemy. The world does not exist in absolute harmony. Wisdom and stupidity go hand in hand, as do fulfilment and failure, kindness and cruelty and importantly for us Christians, life and death. The observation and experience of good and evil through the entire world proves the existence of a spiritual, real, hostile, dynamic power, not motivated by God. Therefore we must understand that the world and perhaps even the astronomical world around us is his domain.

Knowing your Enemy

Although we have touched on the issue of the nature of evil in a previous chapter, it would be worth spending more time on this as we endeavour to understand our eschatological identity and purpose as God's people.

Satan is a fallen angel. He possesses personality. Like his Creator, he has a mind, emotions and an ability to choose. He can communicate as he did with Eve in the Garden of Eden and with Jesus in the wilderness. He has purposes and plans and offered Jesus kingdoms, providing he would compromise. As a result, Satan is held personally accountable to God for his actions.

Why? Why? Why?

When this rebellion is finally put down, nobody will ever question God's authority or that it cannot be taken away from him.

The conflict of these powers is being waged at every level within the universe. It is active in heaven because Satan has access to God; demonic and angelic armies are at war (Job 1:6–12; Dan 10:13; Rev 12:7–9; Rev 12:10). But the universe is also a battleground. Battlegrounds do not choose where the battle is to be fought. The commanders of the armies do. Just as the battle centred upon the Son of God 2,000 years ago, so now the battle centres upon a corporate body of Christ of whom Jesus is the head.

All these are reasons why we must be clear in our thinking and theology, behaviour and speech. There is no virtue in woolly-mindedness and woolly convictions. But we must remember that God resists the proud, yet gives grace to the humble (Jas 4:6).

Did God know?

We now come to the very controversial issue of foreknowledge and predestination. When God created the world, did he foresee all the pain and misery it would contain? If so, as reasonable beings, made in the image of God, we know that knowledge and responsibility are directly related. As knowledge increases, moral responsibilities increase. Evil is not the mere absence of good; good does not exist until a choice for good is made. God is good because he has chosen to be good. God is not just a blob of neutral goodness in the sky. We could not worship someone for being what they *have* to be. We can only worship someone, adore them and revere them because they have chosen to be the way they are.

It is difficult to come to terms with a God who is love when, apparently, he is supposed to have known that the majority of people would go to hell, die of starvation, die of AIDS, suffer untold and innumerable sicknesses and live hell on earth. However, I would like to suggest that choices cannot be known until they are made, as they do not exist until the time they are decided upon. As God does not coerce us in our choices, he cannot be held responsible for them. He simply created the possibility for such choices.

Because God is all-powerful, he can break in at any time: when you are God, you can do things like that! But he gives us an orderly world in which to live. When you abandon God, you abandon God's moral order for society. This order breaks down at every level: relationally, morally, sexually, in government and trade unions, in commerce and industry, with all the spin-offs of sickness and death, decay and disease.

Eliminate choice — say it is all preordained — and you eliminate virtue. Doing right is worthy of congratulation, applause and praise because it implies that wrong could have been done — but was not.

It is very fashionable in certain Christian circles to say 'If we could prove God he would not be God' or 'If we could understand God then we would be equal to him.' Or even 'If we could understand him, he could not be God.' This is of course absurd. It is like saying that if you understand a friend, you become that friend. Or if you understand the workings of a computer, you become a computer. Or a washing machine. Or a television set. God fully understands the principles of human personality, a computer, the washing machine and the television. But he is not a human being, a computer, a washing machine or a television set.

Understanding is essential when it comes to a moral universe where moral creatures have to answer to God. Animals are not accountable to God. They have no sense of moral right and wrong. This is not true of humanity nor the angels and demons. Each is accountable in a moral order to a moral God because they are moral beings. Understanding the truth about God, what God knows and what God says is significant for us all. It determines our view of sin, prayer, evangelism — indeed the whole of life.

Truth is not determined by what you and I experience. God is truth, God is true. Jesus said 'I am the truth', which in the Greek means 'I am the sum total of all reality'. Scripture nevertheless presents God as a living Person who forms definite acts at specific times. He rests and observes, thinks and reasons. He remembers and chooses not to remember. He is able to become grieved, jealous or angry. He is moved with compassion, forgives and comforts, repents and changes his plans and makes new decisions.

Yet we have to say that the only things we know about God are those things which he chooses to reveal to us. God invites us to seek him, talk to him, hunger and thirst after righteousness; he invites us to friendship, to a father-son relationship, to discover, plan and create. God's actions are frequently dependent upon the actions of other people. God is an active participant in the affairs of humanity. He is well able to cope with the challenge of dealing with that which is not yet known. The Spirit of God's kingdom is active — here and now!

Powerful prayer

So — does prayer change things?

As I said at the beginning of this chapter, we should pray as though everything depended on God and work as though everything depended on us. This is good theology.

It is through bodies that God gets his will done in the main, and that is dependent on our response, free choice and willingness to take Scripture seriously. Unless people had chosen to submit to Christ and his word, had paid the price to make things happen, many nations would never have heard the gospel.

However, there are some who believe that prayer is simply a therapy. That is, we may change or improve ourselves through prayer but it is unlikely our circumstances will change. It is simply that we are able to cope better, despite the circumstances. But Jesus talked about moving mountains, and encourages us to use his name in prayer. We are to pray as Jesus would pray in that situation. It is in the name of Jesus people were healed, delivered of demons, raised from the dead (Jn 14:14; Jn 15:7; Lk 11:10; Ps 37:4).

But there are requirements. And all of these have to do with our free choice. These conditions include 'if two of you should agree'; 'delight yourself in the Lord'; 'abide in me'; 'if you ask anything in my name'. God responds to faith.

When entire governments have hounded Christians, persecuted leaders, imprisoned and killed them, we should not be surprised that the absence of God's power, word and people creates a vacuum that demons rush into. Nature abhors a vacuum. Something always fills it. If you remove the light there is only darkness left. If you remove the good, evil will flourish.

Prophetic prayer

As a result of prayer, many events, prophesied in the power of God's Spirit, never happen. King Hezekiah was literally on his death-bed. God spoke to Hezekiah through the prophet Isaiah and his death was foretold. But the King pleaded with God. As a result of this response God heard his prayer, saw his tears and added fifteen years to his life. There are other instances where God changes his mind, turns around; it is called repentance. Repentance is not feeling sorry for something, though that may be involved, but it is the 180 degree turnaround (Josh 3:10; Is 38:1; Judg 3:4–5).

Now how could God add fifteen years to a man's life when he knew he wasn't going to die? Was God threatening him with a death that wasn't going to take place? Impossible! What would we call a doctor who explained to a person that they would be dead within the year if they continued to live a certain way, when the doctor knew full well that even if they continued living like that it wouldn't make the slightest bit of difference? Well, we would hardly call him a good doctor and I doubt whether we would call him moral.

The Bible portrays God as One who thinks sequentially, can act and can do anything he wishes, providing it is consistent with his nature and therefore his word. What an exciting kingdom this is! Scripture explains that God changed his mind, turned around and repented, over thirty times! It does not say that God had poor judgement. It rather shows God's grace, perseverance and willingness to offer mercy, despite humanity disappointing and hurting the Godhead.

God being God can of course cause events to take place in the lives of individuals and even nations. But when Jesus taught his disciples how to pray there were three factors he focused in on. The first is that God wants his good will performed in the earth; the second, that his will is not being done; and the third, that through prayer and action we can do something about getting his will done on the earth.

Our intelligent God gives intelligence to his creation. We can communicate intelligently. Though sin has ruined our receiving apparatus, God's broadcasting apparatus is in perfect condition! So we see in part, prophesy in part, know in part and all of it is tainted with the fallenness of humanity and the sinfulness of the creation around us.

God has communicated to us. He has made contact with humanity. He did this through prophets, priests and kings, but primarily through Jesus Christ. But this communication has been recorded and preserved in writings we call Scripture or the Bible. All logical discoveries within those books must be based on facts. As an archaeologist once commented, 'A fact is an obvious conclusion from recurring evidence, and conclusions from facts must be in harmony.'

The wonderful thing is that recurring evidences concerning God and his purposes are found in thousands of Greek and Hebrew manuscripts. Further thousands of archaeological discoveries confirm events spoken of in Scripture, written material from those who were not even believers who lived in Bible times. There are also the remarkable changes in the lives of millions of believers throughout the world.

So intelligence demands that we look at Scripture seriously. With the help of the Spirit, with revelation from heaven, we can see that our response to God and his word either furthers or hinders an answer to the prayer our Lord taught his disciples.

Prayer and relational unity are vital to evangelism. If we only see evangelism as filling up our church building or notching up church-plants, we fail to understand Scripture.

Other gods?

God never said you should not be an atheist. What he did make clear was that to reject the true God means you now have an opportunity of making another. In fact it has been said by atheists and liberal cynics that God is an invention of humanity. This is absurd. Unbelieving humans don't want God. They certainly don't want the God of truth, a God who cuts across their very nature. It is more convenient to replace him with a lump of stone, a chunk of gold or silver, a wood-carving or simply to embrace a hedonistic life style. Superstition and fantastical ideas abound, but people become very committed to them.

A reason to live

Interestingly enough, Jesus never used the message of the cross or hell to win converts. But many repented, changed their life style and were renewed in their faith in God.

But when Jesus went to the cross, history was about to change — for ever. He refused a liquid to alleviate his sufferings. Almost certainly this was to preserve his faculties in order to carry out his Father's will. It was only later the disciples and apostles realised what was happening. Christ became a substitute, he took our place on the cross. Paul wrote that he preached Christ crucified (1 Cor 1:17). Yet there are major writings from the pen of Paul that never mention the cross. He was, as many Christians are today, speaking of the implications and ramifications of embracing the Christ of Calvary.

It is through the cross that God has reconciled people to himself. It is through the blood of his cross that he has made peace between human beings and heaven (Col 1:20).

But the good news is — the Christ who died is alive! He rose from the dead, he had power to lay down his life and power to take it up again (Jn 10:18). What a staggering moment it must have been for the disciples when they saw him; what drama, what joy, what a laugh! Sadly, a sense of humour, particularly in the pulpit and on platforms, seems to have been surgically removed from evangelical speakers. So, in the power of God's resurrection Spirit, the same Spirit that raised Jesus from the dead, we are told to live in the world but not be saturated with its values and share in its goals. We are to 'render unto Caesar the things that are Caesar's and to God the things that are God's'. But our mission is to stop our Caesar from making off with the lot! It doesn't belong to him.

And yet this resurrection Spirit, while it is bold and powerful, is given by One who was not filled with the wealth, sensuality or beauty of the powerful. It came from One who was like a lamb. What a Saviour!

The moment we are born, we begin to die. Death for most people is extremely unpalatable. Most of us do all we can to put off that day. A godless existence by choice or ignorance affects our outlook on the whole purpose of humanity. I suppose it is inevitable that in a hedonistic, getting, grabbing society like ours, death should seem terrible. If humanity is the most there is in the universe, our existence exhausts the whole content of the human race and our environment. Our death is too outrageous, prolonged and unbearable to be contemplated. So it is better ignored.

Malcolm Muggeridge once quoted Simone de Beauvoir and her book *A Very Easy Death*. In it she described her mother's cancer and subsequent departure as being 'as violent and unforeseen as an engine stopping in the middle of the sky'. For the unbeliever, death is not the final act of an unfolding drama to be followed by a change of scene, but an 'unjustifiable violation', a 'monstrous injustice'. And yet when Dietrich Bonhoeffer was taken by two Nazi guards to the gallows he told them, 'For you it is an end, for me a beginning.'

Hope for the world

We live in a crazy mixture of twentieth-century scepticism and, at the same time, a degree of credulity almost unique throughout history. On the one hand, a people who believe in nothing and trust nobody. On the other, a people who will believe anything — providing it isn't in the Bible.

That is why, as Christians, we should learn from C. S. Lewis who explained that it was one of the favourite devices of the devil to set people arguing about inessentials, in order to take their minds off essentials.

Many people, tired of this wrangling, have ended up staring into newspapers or television screens. Their getting away from it all doesn't change our kingdom mandate to go into God's world and be good news and share that good news wherever we can. Some of us will be called to serve, support, pray and finance those who are out on the front. In one sense we are all out on the front but there is nevertheless a front line even with those who are out on the front.

So, in the power of God's Spirit, moulded by his word, encouraged by his promises, we launch into another situation, another day, another era of our doubts as well as faith, with our fears as well as love. Not superhumans devoid of either. But we embrace our doubts, we work them through. Doubt can be a God-given ability which enables us to come to a knowledge of the truth. In fact the only people I have ever talked to who never doubt are materialists and atheists.

Living in time, we belong to eternity. So what are we going to do with that time? We can only do one thing. And that is be obedient to the King and his kingdom mandate. We could reach our world by the year 2000. At the turn of this century, students in many parts of the world were talking of 'the evangelisation of the world in this generation'. We are now refocusing so that this task is not left in the hands of a few entrepreneurs, orators, television evangelists or Bible translators. But the commission must be absorbed into the hearts and minds of all those — men, women and children — who claim to be followers of Christ and see themselves as a resource for that end.

As the Christian mind is recovered we shall see the crucial importance of God's word and God's words. We shall have what others call a high view of Scripture giving us the revealed body of truth concerning God and his world.

We shall see that we have a gospel which is more than a bunch of words. Past works cannot save us or put us in a better standing with God in terms of our salvation — they are the natural outworking of a life devoted to Christ and his eschatological purposes. Helping the youth in our area, the elderly, the single, lonely and bereaved, or AIDS sufferers through ministries like ACET or the Mildmay Mission — we will show our faith by our works. And many will see their full-time work for the Lord in terms of their business, nine to five daily jobs, as they work well, and take a little bit of heaven into their office, shop, or factory. Full-time work can be secular employment.

And finally, we must pray for a great outbreak of the miracle-working power of God. This will make people wonder about the cause of such healing power and we shall be ready with an intelligent and attractive presentation of Christ and his gospel.

Those who respond to the words, works and wonders, to the Christ of the cross and of the resurrection, will know that in the future the kingdom will come in glorious power when we shall need to sing a new song in a language which we have only been told about. Our role in the meantime is to look forward to that day and ensure that we can get as much as possible of the kingdom — now!

If you put this book down in a few seconds stirred but dissatisfied, challenged but directionless, aspiring but with a sense of terrible limitation, then you are probably a Kingdom person. Hungering, thirsting, asking, seeking — Jesus says those who do these things are Kingdom people. Move on, pay the price, continue the process: the Kingdom of heaven is at hand.

Gerald Coates leads the Pioneer Team, which cares for churches, plants new churches, and trains teachers and evangelists. Pioneer produce a magazine and run a bi-annual conference which attracts several thousand people. For more details, and a copy of the Pioneer Direct mail order catalogue, write to:

Pioneer
PO Box 79c
Esher
Surrey
KT10 9LP

An Intelligent Fire

by Gerald Coates

'I'm sure on the day Gerald was born someone said, "Let the controversy begin". I think that is one of the things I love him for the most!'

—**JOHN WIMBER**

'Brilliant. Controversial. Unpredictable. Quotable. Lovable. That's Gerald.'

—**R. T. KENDALL**

'Gerald is never afraid of ruffling a few feathers. But his outspokenness and quest for the truth are the kind of qualities which are needed by the modern church. When people are looking for values, Gerald never disappoints.'

—**DAVID ALTON, MP**

'Gerald walks like he feels good about himself. He talks like he feels even better about his God and Saviour. He leaves those who see and hear him feeling much the same way.'

—**JEAN DARNELL**

'Gerald is a "one off". We are not likely to see a repeat in this generation! Controversial but caring, he combines a passion for evangelical unity with a commitment to strip the veneer of religiosity from contemporary Christianity. I value his friendship, his wisdom and all the trouble he causes me!'

—**CLIVE CALVER**

'Gerald loves God, loves God's people and loves God's world.'

—**TERRY VIRGO**